Recipes from an Old New Orleans Kitchen

Suzanne Ormond

PELICAN PUBLISHING COMPANY
GRETNA 1988

Copyright © 1988
By Suzanne Ormond
All rights reserved

Artwork by Suzanne Ormond

Library of Congress Cataloging-in-Publication Data

Ormond, Suzanne.
 Recipes from an old New Orleans kitchen.

 1. Cookery, American—Louisiana style. 2. Cookery—
Louisiana—New Orleans. I. Title.
TX715.07354 1988   641.59763   88-12478
ISBN 0-88289-699-7

Manufactured in the United States of America

Published by Pelican Publishing Company, Inc.
1101 Monroe Street, Gretna, Louisiana 70053

NUMBERED LIST OF RECIPES

DRINKS
1. Nectar Ice Cream Soda
2. Chocolate Amaretto Freeze
3. Sangria
4. Strawberry Daiquiris
5. Milk Punch

APPETIZERS
6. Window Pane Sandwiches
7. Cheese Straws
8. Fried Eggplant Fingers
9. Prosciutto with Fresh Figs
10. Sardine Pâté
11. Avocado-Shrimp Canapé
12. Shrimp Crabmeat Quiche
13. Pickled Shrimp
14. Marinated Crab Claws
15. Crabmeat Mousse
16. Cajun Popcorn
17. Angel on Horseback

SOUPS
18. Oyster-Artichoke Soup
19. Cream of Crabmeat Soup
20. Oyster-Shrimp Chowder
21. Bouillabaisse
22. Onion Soup
23. Gazpacho
24. Chilled Avocado-Split Pea Soup
25. Chilled Broccoli Soup
26. Creole Chili Beans
27. Red Bean Soup
28. Turkey Filé Gumbo

ENTREES, MEAT AND FOWL

29. Beef Rib Eye Chez Ormond
30. Meatballs and Sausage
31. Tripe à la Creole
32. Creole Corned Beef Hash
33. Creole Oxtail Stew
34. Creole Baked Beef Brisket
35. Cajun Sausage Kabobs
36. Rock Cornish Hens with Louisiana Brown Rice Dressing
37. Chicken Pecan Rice
38. Chicken Bordelaise
39. Chicken Breasts en Papillote
40. Chicken Livers Véronique
41. Turkey Poulette Roosevelt
42. Honey-Baked Chicken Breasts
43. Sautéed Chicken Breasts
44. Roast Pork Loin with Chestnuts and Prunes
45. Barbecued Spare Ribs
46. Barbecued Short Ribs
47. Veal Rolls Creole

ENTREES, FISH AND SHELLFISH

48. Bronze Catfish
49. Trout Marguery
50. Salmon Croquettes
51. Paella Louisiane
52. Oysters with Vermicelli
53. Oyster Patty Thermidor
54. Crawfish Jambalaya
55. Crawfish Cardinal
56. Crawfish Creole
57. Crawfish Crêpes Roulades
58. Pasta Etouffé
59. Crawfish and Leeks
60. Louisiana Frogs' Legs
61. Shrimp and Mushrooms
62. Shrimp and Tomatoes
63. Hot Crabmeat Ravigote

EGGS
- 64. Crabmeat Omelette
- 65. Scrambled Eggs in Toast Cups
- 66. Eggs with Potato Pancakes
- 67. Eggs in Tomatoes
- 68. Eggs Creole

VEGETABLES
- 69. Stuffed Cabbage
- 70. Candied Carrots
- 71. Onion Soufflé
- 72. Onion Rings
- 73. Baked Onions and Tomatoes
- 74. Creole Tomatoes Pesto
- 75. Grilled Tomatoes
- 76. Potato Balls
- 77. Cauliflower au Gratin
- 78. Creole Stewed Corn
- 79. Brown-Wild Rice Casserole
- 80. Stuffed Eggplant

SALADS
- 81. Mardi Gras Salad
- 82. New Potato Salad
- 83. Coleslaw
- 84. Corn-Tomato Salad
- 85. Avocado with Crabmeat
- 86. Nectarine-Rice Salad
- 87. Seafood Salad
- 88. Shrimp Salad
- 89. Eggplant-Shrimp Salad
- 90. Hot Chicken Salad

DESSERTS
- 91. Pineapple Upside-Down Cake
- 92. Strawberry Shortcake
- 93. Cassata Orleans
- 94. Zabaglione à la Creole
- 95. Brownie Waffles à la Mode
- 96. Praline Parfait

97. Cantaloupe à la Mode
98. Mile High Pie
99. Pineapple-Banana Canapé
100. Peaches in Champagne
101. Fresh Peach Cobbler
102. Grandmother's Omelette Soufflé
103. Yam Pudding
104. Gingerbread
105. Banana-Pecan Bread
106. Honey-Pecan Bread
107. Lemon Ladyfingers

LAGNIAPPE

108. Breakfast Corn Bread Muffins
109. Gingerbread Waffles
110. Garlic Popovers
111. Hush Puppies
112. Muffuletta Sandwich
113. All-Purpose Seasoning
114. Homemade Creole Mayonnaise
115. Creole French Dressing
116. All-Purpose Cajun Barbecue Sauce
117. Pesto Sauce Louisiane
118. Remoulade Sauce Creole
119. All-Purpose Creole Tomato Sauce
120. All-Purpose Sauce Piquante
121. Chocolate Sauce

Preface

THERE ARE WHIMSICAL ghosts who live in our kitchens. They have provided that secret ingredient called spice, or flavor.

First the French and Spanish, in the eighteenth century, came to Louisiana and New Orleans. In the nineteenth and twentieth centuries came Americans, Germans, Irish, Italians, and Latin Americans. Each group brought their recipes with them, and adapted their recipes to the local seafood, vegetables, and fruits. Each group borrowed from the other. The combination of all these cultures has added a very special feeling to Creole-Cajun food and cookery as we know it today. It is hard to say what part is really drawn from which culture—the blend has become that perfect.

This book is an array of recipes gathered from all these cultures. It is the serendipity of bringing together foods that makes Creole-Cajun cooking work. In New Orleans we have Italians cooking Cajun; we have Irish cooking Creole; we have Latin Americans cooking American. It is no wonder that gumbo is our official state dish. There are as many different recipes for gumbo as there are residents in the entire state of Louisiana. With this interchange, it is no surprise that all of the recipes can be good. When we Louisianians are not eating food, we are talking about food.

In the past few years there has been a slight flurry about calories, sodium, and cholesterol, and some attempt has been made to reduce these in many of our famous dishes. Thank goodness, none of the flavor has disappeared. But no matter—we are proud that we create and eat some of the finest food prepared and served anywhere in the world.

SUZANNE ORMOND

ABOUT THE COVER

Courtyard Kitchen of the Hermann-Grima Historic House
820 Saint Louis Street
Vieux Carré, New Orleans, Louisiana

This Creole kitchen is housed in a three-story building. It was built in 1831 by Samuel Hermann and has been restored to its original nineteenth-century appearance, with authentic cooking utensils, open-fire hearth, ovens, and furniture unique to this area and its cuisine. As a working Creole kitchen, it is used for cooking classes and preparing special seasonal menus for holiday celebrations in the nineteenth-century tradition.

The main house and kitchen are owned by the Christian Woman's Exchange, which purchased the property in 1924. The Hermann-Grima Historic House holds the following distinctions:

    National Register of Historic Places (listed)
    National Historic Landmark (listed)
    Certificate of Recognition, Vieux Carré Commission
    50th Anniversary Architectural Award, Vieux Carré
      Commission

The house, kitchen, and stable buildings comprise a historic museum, which is open to the public daily except Sundays.

Recipes
from an Old
New Orleans Kitchen

Drinks

• 1 •
NECTAR ICE CREAM SODA

Nectar syrup (see below)
2 scoops vanilla ice cream
Chilled club soda
1 tablespoon milk

Whipped cream
Old-fashioned soda fountain glass, or 16-oz. tumbler

NECTAR SYRUP

2 cups water
2 cups white sugar
1 14-oz. can sweetened condensed milk

1 teaspoon vanilla extract
1 teaspoon almond extract
1/2 teaspoon red food coloring

Bring water and sugar to a boil in saucepan. Reduce heat and simmer until sugar is dissolved. Remove from heat. Add remaining ingredients. Beat well. Refrigerate. Will keep for 6 weeks.

TO ASSEMBLE: In a tall soda fountain glass or tumbler, put about 4 tablespoons nectar syrup and 1 tablespoon milk. Stir. Fill glass 3/4 full with chilled soda water. Stir. Add 2 scoops vanilla ice cream, and top with whipped cream. Serve with straw and beverage spoon. Serves 1.

• 2 •
CHOCOLATE AMARETTO FREEZE

6 oz. whole milk
1 oz. Amaretto liqueur
2½ tablespoons chocolate syrup

1½ cups cube ice, or 12 large cubes
10-oz. Old-Fashioned glasses

Mix all ingredients in blender at highest speed. Blend for 2 minutes or until ice is completely crushed. Pour into Old-Fashioned glasses. Serve at once with straw. Serves 2.

• DRINKS •

· 3 ·
SANGRIA

1/2 cup orange juice
1/2 cup lemon juice
1/2 cup dissolved white sugar
1 liter, or 4 cups, dry red wine
1/2 cup brandy

1 cup chilled club soda
1½ cups fresh fruit (banana, melon, orange, pineapple, apple, or peach)
4 ice cubes

In large pitcher, pour orange and lemon juice and dissolved sugar. Stir in remaining ingredients. To serve, place some of the fruit in large chilled wine glasses and pour strained liquid over fruit. Serves 6.

· 4 ·
STRAWBERRY DAIQUIRIS

1 cup fresh or frozen whole strawberries
3 oz. light rum
1 tablespoon white sugar

2 teaspoons lime juice
1/2 cup ice, or 6 large ice cubes
8-oz. wine glasses

Mix all ingredients in blender. Mix at highest speed for a few seconds. Mixture should be well blended and fluffy. Pour into wine glasses. Serves 2.

· DRINKS ·

• 5 •
MILK PUNCH

2 cups whole milk
3 oz. brandy or bourbon
2 tablespoons sugar

1/2 cup ice cubes, or about
  6 large cubes
Nutmeg
8-oz. tumblers

Mix first four ingredients in blender. Mix at highest speed for a few seconds. Strain into tumblers and sprinkle with nutmeg. Serves 2.

Appetizers

• 6 •
WINDOW PANE SANDWICHES

12 slices (1/2 inch thick) white bread
2 large tomatoes, very thinly sliced
6 strips bacon, cooked and crumbled

Mayonnaise
Creole mustard
Salt
Paprika

Cut crust from bread. Roll each slice thin with rolling pin. With each of 6 slices of the bread, cut center hole 2 inches in diameter with biscuit cutter. Discard bread circle.

TO ASSEMBLE: Spread mayonnaise and mustard on 6 bottom slices (without center holes). Carefully arrange tomato slices on each bread slice. Sprinkle small amount of salt on tomatoes. Sprinkle crumbled bacon on top. Place top slice with center hole over each bottom slice. Sprinkle with paprika. Serves 6.

• 7 •
CHEESE STRAWS

1 pound sharp cheddar cheese, grated
4 sticks softened margarine
2 teaspoons salt
1 tablespoon Tabasco
1 tablespoon Worcestershire sauce
4½ cups sifted all-purpose flour
1 teaspoon baking powder

Preheat oven to 400°F. Combine all ingredients in food processor or electric mixer. Mix well.

Fit decorating tube with largest opening tube (leaf). Fill tube with cheese mixture. On large cookie sheets (10 × 15 inches), press out strips of dough about 2 inches long. Allow for space between. Bake in oven for 6 to 8 minutes. Do not overbake. Remove straws at once to a cooling rack. Repeat process until all dough is used. Store in tight container. Makes 6 dozen.

• APPETIZERS •

FRIED EGGPLANT FINGERS

3 small eggplants, peeled
1/2 cup flour
1/2 cup yellow corn meal
1 teaspoon cornstarch
2 eggs beaten with 1 tablespoon water

2 tablespoons grated Parmesan cheese
Black pepper and salt
Cooking oil

Cut eggplant into strips, 1/2 × 2 inches. Soak eggplant strips in salted ice water for 30 minutes. Drain eggplant strips. Combine corn meal, flour, cornstarch, salt, pepper, and Parmesan cheese. Dip eggplant strips in corn meal mixture and then in egg mixture. Coat again in corn meal mixture. In large skillet with about 1 inch of oil, heated to 375°F, fry eggplant fingers about 3 to 4 minutes or until golden brown. Drain on absorbent towel. Serve at once. Serves 6.

PROSCIUTTO WITH FRESH FIGS

1/2 pound sliced prosciutto
4 cups fresh figs, peeled

Lemon slices

Divide slices of prosciutto onto 6 salad plates. Each should have 4 to 6 slices. Divide figs evenly and put them on top of prosciutto. Garnish with lemon slices.

NOTE: If fresh figs are not available, a melon cut in slices may be substituted. Serves 6.

• APPETIZERS •

• 10 •
SARDINE PATE

8 oz. sardines, washed of oil
1 stick softened butter
2 tablespoons minced onions
2 tablespoons minced celery
2 tablespoons minced parsley
1/4 cup black olives, coarsely chopped

2 hard-boiled eggs, finely chopped
3 tablespoons fresh lemon juice
4 drops Tabasco
1/8 teaspoon anise seeds

Pick through sardines and discard bones and skin. In food processor, combine sardines, butter, lemon juice, Tabasco, and anise. Mix 3 or 4 seconds until blended. Put sardine mixture in large bowl and combine with all other ingredients. Mix well. Roll in a ball and wrap with waxed paper. Refrigerate for 4 hours. Serve with Melba toast. Makes 3 cups.

• 11 •
AVOCADO-SHRIMP CANAPE

6 slices (1/2 inch thick) white bread
1 large avocado
1 cup boiled shrimp, peeled and deveined

1/2 cup minced celery
1/2 cup minced onions
Salt and pepper to taste
Few drops lemon juice

Chop onions and celery in food processor. In mixing bowl, mash avocado until smooth, and add onions and celery. Set aside. Cut crust from bread, and toast on one side under broiler. Add shrimp and salt and pepper, with lemon juice, to avocado mixture. Fold in shrimp and spread on untoasted side of bread. Serves 6.

• APPETIZERS •

SHRIMP CRABMEAT QUICHE

PASTRY

1 8-inch pie pan
1 cup sifted enriched flour
1/2 teaspoon salt
1/3 cup shortening
3 to 4 tablespoons cold water

Sift flour and salt together in bowl. Cut shortening into flour until small particles appear. Sprinkle cold water over mixture, tossing lightly with fork until dough is moist enough to hold together. Form a ball. Cover ball with waxed paper. Refrigerate for 20 minutes. Roll dough out on floured board to a circle 1½ inches larger than 8-inch pie pan. Fit pastry loosely into pie pan. Fold edges to form a standing rim, and flute.

FILLING

12 medium boiled shrimp, peeled and deveined
1/2 cup cooked white crabmeat
1/4 pound grated Swiss cheese
2 cups milk
3 eggs
1 teaspoon salt
1/16 teaspoon black pepper
1/16 teaspoon Cayenne pepper

Arrange shrimp in bottom of pie shell. Cover with crabmeat. Cover with grated Swiss cheese. Beat eggs slightly with rotary beater. Add milk and seasonings and continue to beat until well blended. Pour milk mixture over crabmeat, shrimp, and cheese in pie shell. Bake in hot oven (400°F) for 35 minutes or until custard appears firm. Do not overbake. Cool on wire rack for 10 minutes before serving. Serves 6.

• APPETIZERS •

PICKLED SHRIMP

2 pounds shrimp, peeled and deveined
1 medium white onion, sliced
1/4 cup liquid crab boil
3 cups white vinegar
2 tablespoons mixed pickling spice

1 cup water
2 tablespoons sugar
6 large bay leaves
2 cloves garlic, sliced
1 lemon, sliced
1-quart Mason jar with rubber lid

In saucepan, bring shrimp, liquid crab boil, vinegar, sugar and water to boil. Lower heat. Simmer for 5 minutes. Remove from heat and cool slightly. Strain shrimp. Reserve liquid. In bottom of jar, place lemon slices, onions, garlic, and 2 bay leaves. Place layer of shrimp over. Add a teaspoon of pickling spices. Repeat procedure until all ingredients have been used. Pour reserve liquid over. Make sure to cover. If not enough liquid remains, add water. Seal jar tightly. Refrigerate for 4 days before serving. Serve with Melba toast or crackers as an hors d'oeuvre or cold appetizer. Serves 6.

MARINATED CRAB CLAWS

1 pound crab claws
1 cup stale beer
4 cloves garlic, minced
1/2 cup olive oil
1 small onion, puréed

6 drops Tabasco
1/2 teaspoon celery seeds
1/2 teaspoon salt
1/8 teaspoon dried thyme leaves

In large bowl, separate crab claws. Put all other ingredients in blender, and blend on medium speed for 10 seconds. Pour marinade over crab claws and refrigerate for 4 hours, covered loosely with aluminum foil. Serve chilled. Serves 6.

• APPETIZERS •

• 15 •
CRABMEAT MOUSSE

1 cup fresh crabmeat
2 tablespoons dry sherry
1/2 cup very hot chicken broth
2 beaten egg yolks
3 tablespoons unflavored gelatin
1/4 teaspoon Worcestershire sauce

1 teaspoon ketchup
1/2 teaspoon salt
1 tablespoon each, minced onion, parsley, celery
Dash of ground thyme
1/2 cup Creole mayonnaise
1/2 cup heavy cream
2 egg whites, beaten very stiff

Into container of electric blender, put egg yolks, gelatin, sherry, and very hot chicken broth. Cover and blend at high speed for 30 seconds. Add crabmeat, Worcestershire sauce, onion, celery, parsley, thyme, and ketchup. Cover. Blend for 30 seconds. Uncover and add mayonnaise, salt, and cream. Blend for 15 seconds. Pour blended mixture over beaten egg whites and fold in gently. Pour into 1-quart mold and refrigerate for 4 hours. Serve with toasted French bread. Serves 6.

• 16 •
CAJUN POPCORN

2 pounds crawfish tails
Cooking oil

BATTER

3/4 cup sifted flour
1/2 teaspoon baking powder
1 beaten egg
1/2 teaspoon seasoned salt

1/4 teaspoon black pepper
1/2 cup milk
4 drops Tabasco

Beat milk and egg together. Add all other batter ingredients. Mix well. In deep skillet or deep fryer, heat about 4 inches cooking oil to 375°F. Place crawfish tails in batter, coating well. With slotted spoon, draw out coated crawfish tails. Shaking off excess batter, gently separate crawfish. Drop handfuls into hot oil. Deep fry until golden. Remove with slotted spoon and drain on absorbent paper. Repeat process until all tails have been fried. Serve in bowl in same manner as popcorn, as cocktail appetizer. Serves 6.

ANGEL ON HORSEBACK

36 medium oysters, drained
Sliced bacon
Pepper
Lemon wedges

Pepper and wrap each oyster in sliced bacon. Secure with toothpick. Heat heavy skillet. Gently sauté oysters until crisp. Drain on absorbent paper. Serve with lemon wedges as an hors d'oeuvre or hot appetizer. Serves 6.

Soups

OYSTER-ARTICHOKE SOUP

1 quart fresh oysters
3 cans artichoke hearts (about 30)
8 green onions, finely chopped
4 tablespoons butter
4 tablespoons flour
8 cups chicken stock
2 cloves garlic, mashed
1/2 teaspoon crushed red pepper
1 teaspoon salt
1/4 teaspoon black pepper
1 teaspoon thyme leaves
2 teaspoons Worcestershire sauce

Drain oysters in colander and reserve liquor. Wash and drain artichoke hearts and cut each in 4 pieces. Cut oysters in three pieces. In 4-quart saucepan, sauté onions in butter until limp. Add artichoke hearts and continue to cook, but do not brown. Add flour, and blend. Add all other ingredients except oysters and liquor. Bring to boil. Reduce heat to simmer, and cook for 20 minutes. Add oysters and liquor. Return to a boil, reduce heat to simmer, and cook for 15 minutes. Serves 8.

CREAM OF CRABMEAT SOUP

1/2 pound crabmeat
4 chopped green onions
4 tablespoons butter
2 beaten egg whites
4 cups chicken stock
4 tablespoons light cream
1 teaspoon cornstarch
1 tablespoon dry sherry
1/4 teaspoon salt
3 drops Tabasco
2 tablespoons chopped parsley

In 2-quart saucepan, melt butter and sauté green onions for about 1 minute. Add crabmeat, salt, Tabasco, and sherry and cook for 1 minute more. Add chicken stock and stir. Continuing to stir, bring soup to rapid boil. Lower heat to simmer. In small bowl, combine cornstarch and egg whites with cream. Blend well. Add 2 tablespoons of hot soup. Blend until smooth. Add cream mixture to soup mixture. Garnish with parsley. Serves 6.

OYSTER-SHRIMP CHOWDER

24 large oysters
1/2 pound shrimp, peeled and deveined
1 large onion, chopped
4 green onions, chopped
3 large white potatoes, peeled, parboiled, and diced in 1/2-inch cubes
1 cup chopped celery (ribs and tops)
2 tablespoons chopped parsley
3 slices bacon, cooked and crumbled
3 tablespoons margarine
2½ cups milk
1 cup hot chicken broth
1 tablespoon flour
1/2 teaspoon salt
1/8 teaspoon black pepper
1/8 teaspoon thyme leaves
6 drops Tabasco
Oyster crackers

In 3-quart saucepan, sauté onion, green onions, and celery in margarine. Cook about 5 minutes. Add shrimp and cook until pink. Lower heat to medium. Add flour, stirring to blend flour completely. Add chicken broth and cook for 5 minutes. Add parsley, bacon, and potatoes. Stir. Add milk, pepper, salt, thyme, and Tabasco. Lower heat to simmer. Stir. Continue to cook for 15 minutes or until potatoes are tender. Add oysters and stir. Cook until oysters begin to curl at edges, about 5 minutes. Serve at once with oyster crackers. Serves 6.

BOUILLABAISSE

1/2 pound filet of red snapper, cut in 1-inch slices
1/2 pound filet of trout, cut in 1-inch slices
1/2 pound crawfish tails
1/2 pound shrimp, peeled and deveined
1/2 pound crabmeat
4 tablespoons unsalted butter
2 large tomatoes, peeled and finely chopped
1 large onion, finely chopped
3 cloves garlic, mashed
1/4 cup chopped parsley
2 bay leaves
1/2 teaspoon thyme leaves
1/2 teaspoon salt
1/4 teaspoon black pepper
6 drops Tabasco
Water
French bread

In large soup kettle, lightly sauté tomatoes, onions, garlic, and parsley in butter for about 3 minutes. Put fish slices over vegetables. Cover with water and bring to rapid boil. Stir and cook for 15 minutes. Add crawfish tails, crabmeat, shrimp, thyme, bay leaves, salt, pepper, and Tabasco. Stir. Lower heat to simmer and continue to cook for another 15 minutes or until shrimp are done. Remove bay leaves. Serve soup in large soup bowls with French bread on the side. Serves 8.

ONION SOUP

4 large white onions, peeled and thinly sliced
4 cups beef bouillon
4 cups water
3 tablespoons unsalted butter
1 tablespoon flour
1 teaspoon salt
1/4 teaspoon black pepper
French bread slices, toasted
Grated Parmesan cheese

In large saucepan, sauté onions in butter very, very slowly, until onions are soft and golden. Sprinkle flour over onions and blend well. Pour water and beef bouillon over onions and stir well until soup comes to rapid boil. Reduce heat and cover. Simmer for 30 minutes. Season with salt and pepper. Pour soup into ovenproof casserole or individual onion soup dishes. Cover with toasted French bread, and sprinkle generously with grated Parmesan cheese. In 450°F oven, cook until cheese is melted. Serves 6.

GAZPACHO

6 large ripe Creole tomatoes, peeled, seeded, and finely chopped
1/2 cup chopped green onions
1/4 cup white onion, finely chopped
1 green sweet pepper, finely chopped
2 small cucumbers, peeled and coarsely chopped
1/2 cup celery, finely chopped
1/4 cup minced parsley
3 cups tomato juice
1/4 cup olive oil
4 tablespoons lemon juice
1/2 teaspoon salt
1/8 teaspoon black pepper
8 drops Tabasco
1/2 teaspoon garlic salt

In large glass salad bowl or similar large bowl, put tomatoes, green onions, white onion, green pepper, cucumbers, celery, and parsley. Stir them together. In separate bowl, blend tomato juice, lemon juice, olive oil, and seasonings with wire whisk or fork until well blended. Pour over vegetables and chill for 4 to 6 hours. Serve in chilled soup bowls. Serves 8.

CHILLED AVOCADO–SPLIT PEA SOUP

2 large ripe avocados
1/2 pound dried green split peas
1 ham hock
1 large onion, chopped
4 carrots, peeled and coarsely chopped
1/2 cup chopped celery (ribs and tops)
1 clove garlic
2 bay leaves
1 teaspoon salt
1/4 teaspoon pepper
1/4 teaspoon thyme leaves
6 cups water
1½ teaspoons lemon juice
1½ teaspoons Worcestershire sauce
Dry sherry

In colander, rinse and sort peas. Into 3-quart saucepan, put peas, ham hock, onions, celery, carrots, garlic, bay leaves, thyme leaves, salt, and pepper. Cover with water. Bring to boil and stir. Reduce heat to simmer and stir again.

Cover saucepan and cook for 2 hours or until done. Remove bay leaves and ham hock. In food processor, or with coarse food strainer, purée soup until smooth and thick. Return split pea soup to saucepan. Peel avocados and remove and discard pits. Using food processor or coarse strainer, purée avocados until smooth. Combine puréed avocados with split pea soup and blend well. Chill mixture for 4 hours in covered saucepan. Serve in soup bowls with 1/4 teaspoon each lemon juice and Worcestershire sauce per bowl. Garnish with splash of dry sherry. Serves 6.

CHILLED BROCCOLI SOUP

2 cups cooked broccoli
1 small onion, cut in half
1 clove garlic
1/2 cup water
1/2 teaspoon salt
3 drops Tabasco
1 cup chicken stock
1/2 cup half-and-half cream

In blender, put onion, water, garlic, salt, and Tabasco. Blend until smooth. Add broccoli and blend. Pour into bowl and whisk in stock and cream. Cover and refrigerate for 4 hours. Serves 6.

CREOLE CHILI BEANS

4 cups cooked red beans
1 pound lean ground beef
1 large onion, chopped
3 cloves garlic, minced
2½ cups tomato juice
3 tablespoons chopped parsley

5 tablespoons chili powder
1 teaspoon salt
1/2 teaspoon black pepper
6 drops Tabasco
2 tablespoons cooking oil

In 5-quart soup pot, brown beef in cooking oil. Add onions and continue to cook until onions are soft. Add minced garlic and parsley. Add cooked red beans and tomato juice. Stir to blend thoroughly. Add salt, pepper, Tabasco, and chili powder, and stir to mix seasonings thoroughly. Bring to boil. Reduce heat to lowest heat setting possible. Cover pot and continue to cook for 45 minutes. Serve in large soup bowls. Serves 10.

RED BEAN SOUP

4 cups cooked red beans
3 hard-boiled eggs, chopped
3 tablespoons dry sherry

4 tablespoons chopped green onions
Water

In food processor, blend red beans until smooth. In 3-quart saucepan, combine water and red beans to make a thick soup. Bring soup to boiling point and lower heat to a slight simmer. Cook about 5 minutes. Add sherry and garnish with chopped green onions and chopped egg. Serve at once. Serves 6.

TURKEY FILÉ GUMBO

1 carcass roasted turkey with meat on bones

Water

In large soup pot, put turkey carcass and cover with water. Put top on and boil for about 1 hour or until meat falls from bones. Cool. Drain broth and strain. Reserve broth for gumbo. Pick through meat, discarding bones and skin. Chop meat in 1/2-inch cubes.

GUMBO

4 cups turkey meat
1 pound smoked sausage, sliced 1/2 inch thick
1 pound fresh or frozen shrimp, peeled and deveined
3 tablespoons flour
3 tablespoons cooking oil
1 cup finely chopped celery
1/2 cup minced parsley
1 large onion, finely chopped
1 teaspoon salt
1/2 teaspoon crushed red peppers
1/4 teaspoon black pepper
1/4 teaspoon thyme leaves
3 bay leaves
12 cups reserved turkey broth
Filé powder
Boiled white rice (about 3 cups)

In large soup pot, make roux with oil and flour. Brown roux until a rich dark brown. Add broth and all other ingredients except turkey meat, shrimp, rice, and filé. Cover pot. Bring to boil. Lower heat to soft rolling boil. Cook for 30 to 45 minutes. Add turkey meat and shrimp. Continue to cook for 15 minutes. Correct gumbo for salt and black pepper.

Serve in large soup bowls with 1/2 cup rice sprinkled with 1/8 teaspoon filé powder. Ladle hot gumbo over rice. Serve with fresh green salad and lots of hot French bread. Serves 6 to 10.

Entrees
Meat & Fowl

BEEF RIB EYE CHEZ ORMOND

8 to 10 pound boneless beef rib eye
1 pound sliced bacon
12 cloves garlic, peeled
3 tablespoons Kitchen Bouquet
2 teaspoons salt
1 teaspoon black pepper
2 tablespoons cooking oil
Water

With paper towel, thoroughly clean roast. With sharp pointed knife, make 12 deep, evenly spaced cuts on top side of roast. Press a clove of garlic deeply into each cut. Mix Kitchen Bouquet, salt, pepper, and cooking oil in small bowl. With pastry brush, completely coat roast with mixture. Place roast on rack in shallow roasting pan. Layer bacon on top of roast, making sure entire top is covered. Secure bacon with toothpicks. Pour about a cup of water in bottom of pan. Preheat oven to 350°F. Roast 18 minutes to the pound for rare, 22 minutes for medium, 25 minutes for medium well. A meat thermometer may be used, placed in center of fleshy part. Do not allow pan to dry out. Add extra water when necessary. Remove from oven when desired doneness is achieved.

Put all drippings in a separating cup. Remove and discard fat liquid. Retain dark brown drippings. In small saucepan, add 2 parts water for every part drippings. Bring to boil. Reduce heat and keep warm for gravy. Allow roast to rest for 30 minutes before carving. Serves 8 to 12.

MEATBALLS AND SAUSAGE

1 pound lean ground beef
1 pound smoked sausage, sliced 1/2 inch thick
1/4 cup yellow corn meal
1 large beaten egg
2 cloves garlic, minced
1 small yellow onion, puréed
1¼ teaspoons salt
1/2 teaspoon black pepper
Flour
Cooking oil
1 pound boiled macaroni, drained, buttered and kept warm

Mix beef with corn meal, beaten egg, garlic, onion, salt, and pepper. Form into 1-inch balls. Roll in flour. Brown meatballs and sausage in heavy skillet with 1/4 inch cooking oil. Remove and drain on absorbent paper.

GRATED PARMESAN CHEESE SAUCE

Grated Parmesan cheese
1 tablespoon cooking oil
1 small onion, chopped
2 tablespoons chopped parsley
2 cloves garlic, minced
1 tablespoon chili powder
3 cups tomato juice
1/2 teaspoon salt
6 drops Tabasco

Heat oil in large saucepan. Sauté onions until limp. Add all other sauce ingredients except Parmesan. Bring to boil. Lower heat to simmer. Cook for 10 minutes. Drop meatballs and sausage in hot sauce. Cook for 8 to 10 minutes or until sausage is tender. Serve over hot buttered macaroni. Garnish with Parmesan cheese. Serves 6.

• ENTREES, MEAT AND FOWL •

TRIPE A LA CREOLE

1 pound fresh tripe **Water**

Cover tripe with water in large pot. Bring to boil. Lower heat to simmer, and cook for 2 hours or until tripe is tender. Drain. Cut in 2-inch squares.

SAUCE

3 tablespoons cooking oil
3 tablespoons flour
1/2 green pepper, chopped
1½ cups peeled and chopped tomatoes
1 medium onion, chopped

1 large bay leaf
1 teaspoon salt
1/4 teaspoon black pepper
1 cup water
4 drops Tabasco

In covered skillet, make a brown roux with flour and oil. Add onions, green pepper, and tomatoes. Lower heat. Stir until coated. Add water. Stir well to blend. Add salt, pepper, Tabasco, and bay leaf. Cover. Cook for 10 minutes. Remove cover and add tripe. Stir well. Bring mixture back to simmer. Continue to simmer for 15 minutes. Serve over hot buttered boiled grits. Serves 6.

CREOLE CORNED BEEF HASH

2 pounds cooked corned beef, shredded or chopped
5 medium potatoes, cooked, peeled, and diced
3 ribs celery, finely chopped
1 cup minced onion
1/4 cup minced parsley
1 clove mashed garlic

1 large green pepper, seeded and chopped
3 tablespoons butter
1/2 cup beef stock
1 tablespoon Worcestershire sauce
Salt and black pepper to taste
6 poached eggs

In large skillet, sauté onion, green pepper, celery, and garlic in butter until limp. Add corned beef, potatoes, and parsley. Sprinkle Worcestershire sauce over mixture and stir. Lower heat to medium and add beef stock a little at a time, stirring constantly to prevent sticking. Correct seasoning with salt and pepper.

• ENTREES, MEAT AND FOWL •

Transfer mixture to large buttered skillet. Brown on one side. Turn. Make 6 wells in corned beef, evenly spaced. Put a poached egg in each well. Continue to cook for 5 minutes or until bottom is browned. Slide corned beef hash onto serving platter. Serve with hot buttered grits. Serves 6.

CREOLE OXTAIL STEW

2 large oxtails, disjointed
3 tablespoons cooking oil or bacon drippings
1 large onion, sliced
Flour
2½ cups water
1 tablespoon tomato paste
2 tablespoons cider vinegar
1 beef bouillon cube
1 teaspoon salt
1/4 teaspoon each, black pepper and crushed red pepper
1 bay leaf
4 large carrots, peeled and sliced
1 cup thinly sliced celery
1 large green pepper, chopped
5 medium potatoes, peeled and cut in half

Heat oil or bacon drippings in large skillet with cover. Coat oxtails with flour. Brown onion slices and oxtails. Add water, salt, peppers, bouillon cube, tomato paste, vinegar, and bay leaf. Bring to boil. Lower heat to simmer. Cover tightly and cook for 2½ to 3 hours. Add extra water if necessary. Add vegetables. Discard bay leaf. Cover and continue to cook at simmer point for 45 minutes. Add extra water if gravy becomes too thick. Serves 6.

• 34 •
CREOLE BAKED BEEF BRISKET

1 4-pound boneless beef
   brisket, trimmed
3 large onions, peeled and
   sliced
1/4 teaspoon ginger

2 tablespoons cooking oil
1 teaspoon garlic salt
3 tablespoons tomato paste
Salt and black pepper
Extra heavy aluminum foil

Generously salt and pepper brisket roast. Make paste of tomato paste, ginger, garlic salt, and cooking oil. With pastry brush, coat entire roast with paste. Use enough aluminum foil to make cover for entire roast, with extra for butcher wrap, and to make tight ends. Place coated roast in center of foil, and arrange onion slices on top. Fold up foil. Make butcher wrap and secure ends. Place roast in pan large enough to accommodate it. Roast in 350°F oven for 4 hours or 1 hour per pound. Serves 6.

• 35 •
CAJUN SAUSAGE KABOBS

2 pounds Louisiana smoked
   sausage, sliced 1½ inches
   thick to make 36 pieces
1 large green pepper, cut into
   1-inch squares

24 cherry tomatoes
24 large pimiento-stuffed olives
6 10-inch metal skewers

BASTING SAUCE

1 cup stale beer
1/4 cup ketchup

4 drops Tabasco

Blend sauce ingredients well. In large skillet, cook sausage over medium heat until partially cooked. Remove and drain on absorbent paper.

TO ASSEMBLE: Preheat broiler for 10 minutes. Arrange kabob ingredients on skewers and place on cookie sheet. Baste with sauce. Broil 6 inches from heat for 3 minutes. Turn, baste, and broil for 3 minutes. Turn, baste, and broil again for 3 minutes. Remove from broiler and cool slightly. Serve at once. Serves 6.

• ENTREES, MEAT AND FOWL •

ROCK CORNISH HENS WITH LOUISIANA BROWN RICE DRESSING

3 large Rock Cornish hens, split in half

2 tablespoons butter
Salt, pepper and flour

Wash hens and pat dry. Generously salt and pepper halves. Coat well in flour. In heavy skillet, melt butter. Brown hens in butter to golden color. Remove from skillet.

DRESSING

2 cups brown rice
6 cups water
1 teaspoon salt
1/2 cup chopped celery
1 large onion, chopped

3 tablespoons butter
3 tablespoons minced parsley
1/2 teaspoon thyme leaves
1/2 cup chopped pecans
3 slices bacon, cut in halves

In 8-cup saucepan, bring water to boil. Add rice and salt. Stir. Boil rice rapidly for 20 minutes, stirring every 5 minutes, or until just barely done. Drain. In skillet, melt 3 tablespoons butter. Sauté onion, celery, and parsley until limp. Add cooked rice, pecans, and thyme leaves. Toss well. Correct seasoning.

TO ASSEMBLE: Put rice mixture into shallow baking dish. Put browned hen halves over rice. Place a half slice of bacon on top of each hen half. Roast in 450°F oven for 15 minutes. Lower heat to 350°F and continue to roast for 30 minutes or until meat tests done. Serves 6.

· 37 ·
CHICKEN PECAN RICE

1 whole chicken breast, skinless and boneless
7 oz. Wild Pecan Rice (Konriko)
2 chicken bouillon cubes
4 chopped green onions
5 ribs celery with tops, chopped
2 tablespoons minced parsley

1 large tomato, peeled and coarsely chopped
2 tablespoons corn oil
1/2 cup chopped pecans
Black and red pepper and salt to taste

In saucepan, poach chicken breast with enough water to cover. Bring water to boil and put chicken bouillon cubes in. Lower heat and simmer about 15 minutes. Remove chicken and reserve stock.

In 2-quart saucepan, bring 3 cups water to a boil. Pour in rice and stir. Lower heat to simmer and cover. Cook rice about 20 minutes or until almost done. Drain rice in colander and refresh with cold water.

In large skillet, sauté onions and celery in corn oil until limp. Add tomato and parsley. Continue to cook until soft. Cut chicken into 1/2-inch cubes and add to vegetables. Mix in rice and pecans. Lower heat. Add 1/2 cup of reserve stock. Season with salt and peppers. Mix again. Cover and steam for 15 minutes. Serves 6.

· 38 ·
CHICKEN BORDELAISE

3 1½-pound spring chickens, cut in half lengthwise
2 tablespoons butter
2 tablespoons flour
2 cups chicken consomme
6 cloves garlic, very finely chopped

1 medium onion, minced
2 tablespoons minced ham
2 tablespoons minced parsley
8 drops Tabasco
1 bay leaf
1/2 cup dry sherry
Salt and pepper

Salt and pepper chicken and place in shallow dish. Melt butter in skillet. Stir in flour until lightly browned. Add all other ingredients except chicken and sherry, and simmer for 8 minutes. Strain sauce and add sherry. Pour sauce over chicken and allow to marinate for 2 hours. Strain sauce and reserve for basting.

· ENTREES, MEAT AND FOWL ·

Chicken may either be grilled outdoors or in a broiler pan placed 7 to 9 inches below the heat. If chicken is done under broiler, allow 15 minutes on each side. Broil for 1 hour or until done. If outdoor grill is used follow instructions for chicken. Baste chicken frequently. Serves 6.

CHICKEN BREASTS EN PAPILLOTE

3 large breasts of chicken, boneless and skinless, each cut in half
16 oz. beer
2 tablespoons butter plus 4 drops cooking oil
2 tablespoons chopped celery
2 tablespoons chopped onions
1 cup fresh sliced mushrooms
2 green onions with tops, chopped
2 cloves garlic, minced
1/8 teaspoon nutmeg
1/8 teaspoon ground thyme
Salt and black pepper
6 pieces heavy aluminum foil, 8 × 10 inches each
Butter

Place large chicken breasts in large skillet, and cover with beer. Poach chicken for 15 minutes. Remove from heat and cool in broth.

In another skillet, sauté celery, onions, mushrooms, green onions, and garlic in butter and oil for 5 minutes or until slightly tender. Add nutmeg and thyme and blend thoroughly. Remove from heat.

Remove chicken from broth and generously salt and pepper on all sides. Butter aluminum foil pieces, and place a piece of chicken breast on each piece. Cover each breast with sautéed vegetables. Seal up foil pieces, and secure corners tightly.

Place chicken bundles in shallow baking dish. Cook in 450°F oven for 35 minutes. Open foil carefully, allowing steam to escape slowly. Serve at once. Serves 6.

• 40 •
CHICKEN LIVERS VERONIQUE

2 pounds chicken livers
6 tablespoons butter
1/8 teaspoon olive oil
1/2 pound seedless white grapes, washed and stems removed

3/4 cup port wine
Salt and pepper
3 cups boiled brown rice

Wash and drain chicken livers. Salt and pepper them. Melt butter and olive oil together in heavy skillet. Sauté chicken livers until firm and well cooked. Remove to platter and arrange grapes into livers. Deglaze skillet with port wine, scraping sides and bottom clean of brown bits. Reduce to half. Pour sauce over chicken livers and grapes. Serve with brown rice. Serves 6.

• 41 •
TURKEY POULETTE ROOSEVELT

6 large slices (1/2 inch thick) white meat of roasted turkey
6 slices (1/4 inch thick) white bread, toasted and crust removed

12 strips crisply fried bacon

POULETTE SAUCE

4 tablespoons butter
4 tablespoons flour
2 cups hot chicken stock
Salt and white pepper to taste
1/8 teaspoon nutmeg
2 beaten eggs

2 teaspoons lemon juice
1 tablespoon cream or milk
1/2 cup mushrooms, cooked and sliced
1/3 cup grated Parmesan cheese

In 4-cup saucepan, blend together butter and flour to make a roux. Stir with wooden spoon until roux thickens. Do not brown. Lower heat. In a steady stream, add hot chicken stock. Whisk together until smooth and sauce starts to bubble. Remove from heat. Beat in all other sauce ingredients. Correct seasoning.

• ENTREES, MEAT AND FOWL •

TO ASSEMBLE: Put toasted bread in shallow 9 × 13-inch baking dish. Cover each slice with turkey meat. Cover each turkey slice with 2 strips bacon. Pour poulette sauce over turkey and bacon. Smooth with rubber spatula to cover evenly. Preheat broiler. Broil for 4 minutes, about 6 inches from heat or until sauce bubbles. Serves 6.

• 42 •

HONEY-BAKED CHICKEN BREASTS

6 large chicken breasts
1/2 teaspoon salt
1 cup honey
3/4 cup apple cider

1/2 teaspoon dry mustard
Salt and pepper
Cooking oil

Wash and drain chicken breasts. Pat dry with towel. Salt and pepper chicken breasts. Brown chicken breasts in large skillet with just enough cooking oil to cover bottom. Remove. In shallow baking dish, arrange chicken breasts, skin side up. Mix together honey, 1/2 teaspoon salt, apple cider, and mustard, and pour over chicken breasts. In 450°F oven, cook chicken for 10 minutes. Turn chicken. Lower temperature of oven to 350°F. Cover chicken with foil and continue to bake another 25 minutes or until done. Serves 6.

• 43 •

SAUTEED CHICKEN BREASTS

6 large chicken breasts
1/2 stick butter
3 drops cooking oil
1/2 cup lemon juice

1/2 cup dry white wine
1/4 cup minced parsley
Salt, pepper, flour

Wash chicken breasts and pat dry. Generously salt and pepper breasts and dredge them in flour.
    In large skillet with cover, melt butter and oil to bubbling point. With skin side down, brown chicken. Turn. Lower heat. Cover. Steam chicken for 25 minutes or until done.
    Remove chicken to serving platter, and deglaze pan with lemon juice, white wine, and parsley, scraping sides and bottom clean of brown bits. Reduce liquid slightly. Pour sauce over chicken breasts.
    Serve with warm buttered rice. Serves 6.

• ENTREES, MEAT AND FOWL •

ROAST PORK LOIN WITH CHESTNUTS AND PRUNES

1 4-pound boneless pork loin
6 cloves garlic
1 tablespoon cooking oil
1 tablespoon Kitchen Bouquet
1/2 teaspoon ground thyme
1/2 teaspoon ground sage
1 teaspoon salt
1/2 teaspoon black pepper

Make deep slash on top of roast. Insert whole garlic clove. Repeat process until all garlic is used. Mix together all other ingredients. Brush over all sides of pork roast. Place roast on rack in roasting pan. Do not use water in pan. Roast 35 minutes to the pound at 350°F.

CHESTNUTS AND PRUNES

1 pound chestnuts in shells
2 pounds dried prunes
Water
2 bay leaves
1 cup dry white wine
2 tablespoons sugar
1/4 teaspoon ground cinnamon
1 tablespoon butter

Make deep slash on bottom side of each chestnut. Place chestnuts in shallow baking dish. Roast for 30 minutes at 350°F or until shells slip off easily. Chop chestnut meats coarsely. Place prunes in saucepan. Cover with water. Add bay leaves and cinnamon. Bring to boil. Reduce heat and simmer for 15 minutes. Drain. Discard bay leaves. Remove prune pits and chop prunes coarsely. Put butter, sugar, and white wine into a saucepan. Add chestnuts and prunes. Toss well. Simmer for 10 minutes. Serve warm with pork loin. Serves 6.

BARBECUED SPARE RIBS

1 3- to 4-pound rack of spare ribs
Water
4 cloves garlic
1/2 tablespoon salt
1/2 teaspoon black pepper
2 bay leaves

In soup kettle, place rack of spare ribs. Cover with water and add garlic, salt, pepper, and bay leaves. Bring to boil. Lower heat to just under a rolling boil. Cover and boil for 20 minutes. Drain. Discard garlic and bay leaves. Cut rack into rib pieces.

• ENTREES, MEAT AND FOWL •

SAUCE

1 medium onion, cut in quarters
1 lemon, sliced
1 cup ketchup
1/2 cup wine vinegar
2 tablespoons brown sugar
1 teaspoon salt
1/3 cup Worcestershire sauce
1 teaspoon chili powder
1 cup water
4 drops Tabasco

Combine all sauce ingredients except lemon slices in blender. Blend for 30 to 45 seconds at high setting, or until contents are smooth and thick.

Arrange ribs in broiler pan. Brush on sauce generously. Add lemon slices. Broil in preheated broiler 6 inches from heat for 8 minutes. Turn spare ribs. Baste. Broil 7 minutes or until ribs are crisp and browned. Serves 6.

BARBECUED SHORT RIBS

4 pounds beef short ribs, cut 3 inches long
2 tablespoons cooking oil
Flour
Salt and pepper

Salt and pepper short ribs. Roll them well in flour. Heat oil in heavy skillet. Brown short ribs on all sides. Transfer short ribs to 4-quart covered casserole.

SAUCE

1 large onion, peeled and cut in quarters
2 large tomatoes, peeled, seeded, and cut in quarters
4 ribs celery with tops, cut in pieces
5 sprigs parsley
2 tablespoons brown sugar
1 teaspoon salt
3 tablespoons Worcestershire sauce
1 teaspoon yellow mustard
1/4 cup lemon juice
1/2 cup water

Put all sauce ingredients in food processor with steel blade. Process until smooth and thick.

Pour sauce over ribs. Cover casserole. Bake in 350°F oven for 1½ to 2 hours or until tender. Serves 6.

VEAL ROLLS CREOLE

2 top round veal steaks (1/4 inch thick)
1 large white onion, thinly sliced
1 large tomato, thinly sliced
2 tablespoons minced parsley
Salt and pepper
Cooking oil
1 cup tomato sauce

Pound steaks with meat mallet until very thin. Generously salt and pepper each side. Cover steaks with slices of tomato. Top tomato with onion rings. Sprinkle parsley over.

Starting from the longest side, carefully roll up meat. Secure ends with toothpicks. Tie each roll in 4 places with string.

Grease shallow baking dish with small amount of cooking oil. Place veal rolls in dish. Cover both rolls with tomato sauce. Bake uncovered in 350°F oven for 1 hour or until meat is firm and tender. Serves 6.

Entrees
Fish & Shellfish

• 48 •
BRONZE CATFISH

2 pounds thin catfish filets
Cooking oil

Lemon wedges

BRONZING MIXTURE

1 teaspoon salt
1 teaspoon paprika
1/2 teaspoon garlic powder
1/2 teaspoon onion powder

1/2 teaspoon Cayenne pepper
1/8 teaspoon black pepper
1/8 teaspoon chili powder

Mix bronzing ingredients in bowl. Wash and dry catfish. Sprinkle fish with bronzing mixture. In large skillet, put just enough oil to cover bottom. Heat oil until first smoke appears. Put catfish in skillet and cook on one side for 3 or 4 minutes, or until a golden bronze; lower heat and turn fish. Continue to cook for 1 minute. Remove from skillet and drain on absorbent paper. Serve with lemon wedges. Serves 6.

• 49 •
TROUT MARGUERY

6 filets of trout
Water
1 large onion, cut in quarters
3 ribs celery
1 large carrot, cut in thirds
5 sprigs parsley

1/2 teaspoon each, rosemary, crushed red pepper, thyme leaves, basil
1 teaspoon salt
1/2 teaspoon black pepper
2 teaspoons garlic salt

Place filets in pan large enough to hold them. Cover with water and add all other ingredients. Bring to boil and lower heat. Poach fish about 8 to 10 minutes or until done. Remove fish carefully to a serving platter and keep warm.

MARGUERY SAUCE

2 cups boiled shrimp, peeled and deveined
2 cups mushroom slices, parboiled
1/2 cup lump crabmeat
4 beaten egg yolks

2 tablespoons tarragon vinegar
2 tablespoons very hot water
1/2 teaspoon salt
1/8 teaspoon white pepper
1 tablespoon lemon juice
1/2 pound melted butter

• ENTREES, FISH AND SHELLFISH •

In double boiler over hot but not boiling water, put vinegar and egg yolks. Beat with wire whisk until smooth. Add salt, pepper, and lemon juice, beating until sauce becomes thick. Add melted butter and water a little at a time until well blended. Remove sauce from water. Fold in shrimp, mushrooms, and crabmeat. Pour over trout and serve at once. Garnish with parsley. Serves 6.

SALMON CROQUETTES

1 1-pound can salmon, or 2 cups cooked fresh salmon
1 cup cubed boiled potatoes
1 egg, beaten well
1 tablespoon minced parsley
1 tablespoon grated onion
1/2 teaspoon salt
1/8 teaspoon Cayenne pepper
1/4 cup cracker crumbs
1/4 cup flour
1 egg beaten with 1 tablespoon water and 1 teaspoon Worcestershire sauce
Cooking oil

Flake fish, removing skin and bones. In mixing bowl, mix fish, potatoes, egg, parsley, onion, salt, and pepper. Shape mixture into croquettes. Put cracker crumbs and flour into shallow dish. Roll croquettes in mixture. Dip croquettes in egg-water-Worcestershire mixture, then again in crumb-flour mixture. Refrigerate for 30 minutes. Fry in deep fat (375°F) until golden brown. Drain on absorbent paper.

SAUCE

2 tablespoons mayonnaise
1 tablespoon fresh lemon juice
1/2 cup ketchup
3 tablespoons chopped pickles
1/8 teaspoon celery salt

Mix mayonnaise with lemon and pickles until well blended. Add all other sauce ingredients and mix well. Serve with croquettes. Serves 6.

PAELLA LOUISIANE

4 chicken thighs
2 large chicken breasts, cut in half
6 tablespoons butter
1 teaspoon olive oil
3 large cloves garlic, finely chopped
2 cups raw rice
4 cups hot chicken stock
1 teaspoon saffron
1/2 teaspoon salt
1/16 teaspoon Cayenne pepper
15 large shrimp, peeled and deveined
12 large oysters
1/2 pound thinly sliced smoked sausage
2 tablespoons chopped parsley
1/2 cup diced pimientos

In large (about 14 inches) skillet, heat butter, olive oil, and garlic. Sauté chicken parts until golden brown. Remove chicken. In remaining butter and juices, fry rice. With wooden spoon, stir rice constantly until rice is golden and light in weight. Stir in hot chicken stock. Add saffron, salt, and pepper. Stir rice to keep it from sticking, until all liquid is absorbed. Rice will be partially cooked. Remove from heat.

Butter paella dish or deep casserole. Place some chicken on bottom and cover with some sausage, shrimp, and oysters. Sprinkle 1 tablespoon parsley over seafood. Add half of pimientos on top. Cover this with half of rice. Repeat process until all chicken, seafood, and sausage has been used. Bake paella in 350°F oven for 45 minutes. Serve with green salad and garlic French bread. Serves 8.

OYSTERS WITH VERMICELLI

3 dozen small oysters, with liquor
1 cup half-and-half cream
2 tablespoons flour
2 tablespoons butter
4 green onions with tops, chopped
3 tablespoons minced parsley
3 tablespoons spinach purée
1/2 teaspoon salt
1/8 teaspoon white pepper
4 drops Tabasco
1 pound curly vermicelli, cooked
Parmesan cheese for garnish

In large saucepan, sauté onions in butter until limp. Add flour and blend well. With wire whisk, add cream and bring to just under boiling point. Reduce heat. Add parsley, spinach, salt, pepper, and Tabasco, whisking to blend sauce. Add oysters and liquor at once. Blend well. Cook about 5 minutes or until oysters begin to curl at edges. Ladle oysters over hot vermicelli and serve at once, with Parmesan cheese as garnish. Serves 6.

OYSTER PATTY THERMIDOR

6 large patty shells
36 small oysters
1 tablespoon butter
1 tablespoon flour
4 green onions, minced
1 cup milk, scalded
1 egg, beaten well
1 teaspoon dry mustard
1/4 teaspoon salt
Pinch of Cayenne pepper
2 tablespoons dry sherry
1/2 cup cracker crumbs

Prepare patty shells by removing top and inside. Preheat oven to 350°F. In skillet, sauté onions in butter for 3 minutes. Add flour and milk, and bring to boil. Allow to cook until slightly thickened. Remove from heat and add mustard, salt, pepper, and sherry. With wire whisk, beat in egg. Return to low heat and add oysters. Bring mixture to simmer, and cook for 5 minutes or until oysters curl. Add cracker crumbs. Put patty shells on cookie sheet. Fill patty shells with oyster mixture. Put pastry top on shells. Bake in preheated oven for 15 minutes or until shells are golden. Serve at once. Serves 6.

CRAWFISH JAMBALAYA

2 pounds crawfish tails
4 large onions, chopped
1 large tomato, peeled, seeded, and finely chopped
1/2 cup chopped green onion tops
1/2 cup chopped celery tops
2 cups raw long-grained rice
1 tablespoon minced parsley
3 cups water
1 bay leaf
Cooking oil
Salt
Red and black pepper to taste

In large, heavy skillet with cover, put enough oil to cover bottom. Sauté onions and celery until limp. Add crawfish tails and water. Heat to simmer and cook about 10 minutes. Add tomato, parsley, green onions, salt, pepper, and bay leaf, and stir. Wash rice and add to vegetable-crawfish mixture. Toss lightly. Cook rapidly until most of water is gone and rice begins to puff. Lower heat; stir. Cover and cook about 15 to 20 minutes or until rice is cooked. Do not overcook. Remove bay leaf before serving. Serves 6.

CRAWFISH CARDINAL

1 pound crawfish tails
4 tablespoons butter
2 cloves garlic, minced
1 medium onion, minced
3 tablespoons minced parsley
2 tablespoons flour
3/4 cup dry white wine
2 tablespoons tomato paste
1/2 cup half-and-half cream
1/2 teaspoon salt
6 slices white bread, toasted and crust removed
3 drops Tabasco
1/8 teaspoon white pepper

In large skillet, melt butter and add onions. Sauté until limp. Add flour and blend. Add wine, parsley, and garlic, and allow wine to reduce. Add crawfish and tomato paste. Stir well. Lower heat to simmer, and cook for 5 minutes. Add salt, pepper, Tabasco, and cream. Continue to stir until mixture thickens. Serve over toasted bread. Serves 6.

• ENTREES, FISH AND SHELLFISH •

CRAWFISH CREOLE

1½ pounds crawfish tails
1 large onion, finely chopped
1 large green pepper, finely chopped
4 ribs celery, finely chopped
2 tablespoons minced parsley
1 large bay leaf
2 cups chopped tomatoes
1 teaspoon Worcestershire sauce
1/2 teaspoon thyme leaves
1/2 teaspoon sugar
3 tablespoons butter
2 tablespoons flour
3/4 teaspoon salt
6 drops Tabasco
3 cups boiled white rice

In large skillet, melt butter over low heat. Sauté onions and celery until limp but not brown. Push to one side and add flour, stirring until brown. Add all other ingredients except crawfish and rice. Stir constantly until mixture thickens and comes to slow boil. Lower heat until mixture simmers. Cover and continue to cook for 35 minutes. Add crawfish to gravy and continue to cook for 15 minutes. Remove bay leaf. Serve crawfish over boiled rice. Serves 6.

CRAWFISH CREPES ROULADES

1 pound crawfish tails
4 green onions with tops, chopped
3 tablespoons chopped parsley
4 tablespoons butter
Salt and pepper

In skillet, melt butter. Sauté crawfish, green onions, and parsley until firm—about 5 minutes. Correct seasoning with salt and pepper. Remove from heat.

CREPE RECIPE

1 cup flour
2/3 cup water
2/3 cup milk
3 large eggs
3 tablespoons melted butter
1/4 teaspoon salt

Put all crêpe ingredients in blender. Blend until smooth and thick—about 1 minute. Allow to set for 15 minutes.

Heat crêpe pan or 6-inch cast-iron skillet until a few drops of water sputter on hot surface. Brush bottom of skillet with butter or cooking oil, coating well. Pour 3 tablespoons of crêpe batter in center. Turn skillet in all directions, spreading batter. Cook for 30 seconds or until brown. Loosen edges with spatula and turn. Cook other side, and remove to wire rack. Repeat until batter is used. Makes 18 crêpes.

TO ASSEMBLE: Place 3 tablespoons crawfish mixture on bottom third of crêpe. Roll into sausage shape. Grease bottom of shallow baking dish with butter. As each crêpe is filled, place it in dish. Repeat until all filling and crêpes are used.

SAUCE

1/2 cup flour
1½ cups milk
4 tablespoons softened butter
1 beaten egg
1/2 cup grated Swiss cheese
1/2 cup mushrooms, cooked and sliced
Salt to taste
3 drops Tabasco

• ENTREES, FISH AND SHELLFISH •

In 2-cup saucepan, whisk together flour and butter over medium heat. Whisk until blended. In a steady stream, add milk, whisking until well blended. Allow to bubble and thicken. Remove from heat. Beat in egg and grated cheese. Fold in mushrooms. Add salt and Tabasco. Blend well.

Pour sauce over crêpes roulades in the shallow dish. Heat in 400°F oven for 15 minutes or until sauce bubbles. Serves 6.

PASTA ETOUFFE

2 pounds fresh or frozen crawfish tails, shelled
6 oz. unsalted butter
1/2 cup crawfish fat if available
1/4 cup flour
2 large onions, chopped
1 large green pepper, chopped
3 ribs celery and tops, finely chopped
3 cloves garlic, minced

White pepper and salt
1/4 teaspoon Cayenne pepper
1 to 2 cups water
1/2 cup heavy cream
1 tablespoon lemon juice
Minced green onions and parsley
1 pound fresh angel hair pasta, cooked

Make medium brown roux with butter and flour. Add onions, green pepper, celery, garlic, and crawfish fat if used. Cook, stirring frequently, until vegetables are tender and light brown—about 30 minutes. Add crawfish tails, seasonings, lemon juice, and heavy cream. Mix well. Gradually add water, according to desired thickness. Bring to boil; lower heat to simmer. Simmer covered until tails are tender. Add green onions and parsley and serve over cooked pasta. Serves 6.

CRAWFISH AND LEEKS

1 pound crawfish tails
1 large green pepper, finely chopped
1 medium onion, finely chopped
4 large leeks with green tops, thinly sliced
3 ribs celery with tops, coarsely chopped
2 tablespoons minced parsley
1 large bay leaf
2 cups tomatoes, peeled and finely chopped
1/8 teaspoon Cayenne pepper
1 teaspoon Worcestershire sauce
1/2 teaspoon sugar
3 tablespoons butter
2 tablespoons flour
1/4 teaspoon thyme leaves
6 drops Tabasco
1/2 teaspoon salt

In large, heavy skillet with cover, melt butter over low heat. Sauté onion and leeks until soft but not brown. Push onion and leeks to one side; add flour, stirring until brown. Add all other ingredients except crawfish. Stir constantly until mixture thickens and comes to slow boil. Lower heat until mixture simmers. Cover and continue to cook for about 30 minutes. In another skillet in just enough cooking oil to cover bottom, lightly sauté crawfish until pink. Add to gravy and continue to simmer for 10 minutes. After removing bay leaf, serve over boiled rice. Serves 6.

• ENTREES, FISH AND SHELLFISH •

LOUISIANA FROGS' LEGS

12 frogs' legs, cut at joint
1 cup flour
1 teaspoon cornstarch
1 teaspoon seasoned salt
1 egg beaten with 1 teaspoon Worcestershire sauce and 3 tablespoons water

2 lemons, cut in wedges
Cooking oil

Wash and drain frogs' legs. Pat dry with towel. Combine flour and cornstarch with seasoned salt in plastic bag. Make egg wash in bowl large enough to accommodate a frog leg. Dip frog leg in egg wash, then shake well in flour mixture. Coat well.

In deep fryer, heat oil to 375°F. Drop frogs' legs in a few at a time. Fry until golden brown. Drain on absorbent paper. Serve with lemon wedges. Serves 6.

SHRIMP AND MUSHROOMS

36 large shrimp, peeled and deveined
12 large cap mushrooms with stems, sliced
2 cups celery with tops, chopped
6 green onions with tops, chopped
3 large cloves garlic, mashed

1/2 tablespoon flour
6 tablespoons corn oil margarine
1 cup dry white wine
1/2 teaspoon seasoned salt
2 drops Tabasco
1 pound cooked and buttered angel hair pasta

In a large skillet, sauté celery, onions, and mushrooms in 3 tablespoons margarine until limp. Sprinkle flour over and blend well. Lower heat. Add shrimp. Stir. Add all remaining ingredients except pasta. Stir well. Raise heat to boil. Lower heat to simmer. Simmer for 10 minutes or until shrimp are firm. Toss in pasta. Coat well. Serve at once. Serves 6.

SHRIMP AND TOMATOES

36 large shrimp, peeled and deveined
3 large tomatoes, peeled and chopped
1 cup celery with tops, chopped
1 medium onion, chopped
3 green onions with tops, chopped
2 cloves garlic, pressed
2 tablespoons parsley, minced

1 cup chicken broth
1 bay leaf
1/4 teaspoon dry sweet basil
6 tablespoons corn oil margarine
1 teaspoon flour
2 tablespoons lemon juice
1/2 teaspoon seasoned salt
2 drops Tabasco
3 cups hot boiled white rice

In a large skillet, sauté onions and celery in margarine until limp. Sprinkle flour over and blend. Add tomatoes. Stir. Continue to sauté until tomatoes are limp. Add shrimp. Stir. Lower heat and add all other ingredients except rice. Stir well. Simmer for 10 minutes or until shrimp are firm. Remove bay leaf and serve over boiled rice at once. Serves 6.

HOT CRABMEAT RAVIGOTE

1 pound fresh white crabmeat
6 slices white bread, toasted and crust removed
2 tablespoons flour
2 tablespoons butter
1/4 teaspoon salt
1/8 teaspoon white pepper

1 cup half-and-half cream
1/2 cup dry white wine
1/4 cup wine vinegar
6 green onions, finely chopped
1 teaspoon each, minced parsley, chives, tarragon
2 tablespoons butter

In saucepan, melt 2 tablespoons butter. Remove from heat and stir in flour. Add salt and pepper and blend well. Return to low heat and gradually add cream, stirring constantly until sauce becomes thick. Remove from heat and add wine, vinegar, and onions. Return to heat and add 2 tablespoons butter. Stir. Add crabmeat, parsley, chives, and tarragon. Blend well. To serve, place slice of toast on each plate and spoon ravigote over. Serve at once. Serves 6.

• ENTREES, FISH AND SHELLFISH •

Eggs

CRABMEAT OMELETTE

1/4 pound fresh crabmeat
2 large beaten eggs
1 green onion, finely chopped
1/2 teaspoon minced parsley
1 tablespoon dry sherry
Salt and pepper to taste
1 tablespoon butter

Sauté onion and parsley in butter in an omelette pan until limp. Add sherry, crabmeat, salt, and pepper. Pour beaten eggs over crabmeat mixture. Lower heat to medium. When edges start to bubble, carefully turn omelette with the help of a spatula. Continue to cook until eggs are set. Serve at once. Serves 2.

SCRAMBLED EGGS IN TOAST CUPS

12 slices (1/4 inch thick) white bread
Butter

Trim crust from each slice of bread. Roll them thin with rolling pin. Butter each side of bread. Press buttered bread into glass custard cups. Preheat oven to 400°F. Bake bread for 15 to 20 minutes or until toasted. Remove from cups. Keep warm.

SCRAMBLED EGGS

10 large eggs
3/4 cup half-and-half cream
1 cup cooked chopped ham
1 cup cooked chopped mushrooms
4 tablespoons butter
1 drop cooking oil
2 drops Tabasco
1/8 teaspoon black pepper
1/2 teaspoon salt
Paprika

In large bowl, beat eggs and half-and-half cream with wire whisk. Beat rapidly until fluffy. Beat in Tabasco, black pepper, and salt.

Melt butter and oil to bubbling point in large skillet. Sauté ham and mushrooms for 2 minutes. Stir in eggs and cook, stirring constantly. Scrape edges of skillet. Do not overcook.

TO ASSEMBLE: Divide scrambled eggs equally among toast cups. Sprinkle tops with paprika. Serves 6.

EGGS WITH POTATO PANCAKES

12 large eggs
1 cup sour cream

6 slices bacon, cooked and
   crumbled

Poach 12 large eggs and keep warm.

PANCAKES

6 raw medium potatoes
1 small onion, grated
2 beaten eggs
3 tablespoons flour

3 drops Tabasco
1 teaspoon salt
3/4 teaspoon baking powder

Pare and then grate raw potatoes in food processor. Let stand 10 minutes, then pour off liquid.

Put drained, grated potatoes in bowl. Stir in 2 beaten eggs, onion, and all remaining pancake ingredients. Mix thoroughly. Heat cast-iron griddle or large skillet and grease well with solid shortening. Drop potato mixture into skillet in pancakes about 3 inches in diameter. Brown on both sides over medium heat. Drain on absorbent paper. Makes 12 pancakes.

TO ASSEMBLE: Place a poached egg on each potato pancake. Top with a teaspoon of sour cream, and sprinkle with crumbled bacon. Serves 6.

EGGS IN TOMATOES

6 large Creole tomatoes
6 large eggs
Parmesan cheese

Salt and pepper
Butter

Cut a thin slice from top of each tomato. Scoop out seeds and pulp. Discard. Put tomato shells into shallow baking dish. Break an egg into each tomato shell. Dot top of each egg with butter. Sprinkle Parmesan cheese, salt, and pepper on top of each egg. Bake in 350°F oven for 15 minutes or until eggs are set. Serves 6.

EGGS CREOLE

12 large eggs, poached

3 English muffins, halved, toasted, and buttered

In large baking dish, arrange toasted English muffin halves. Cover each muffin half with 2 poached eggs. Keep warm.

SAUCE

3 small tomatoes, peeled and finely chopped
3 tablespoons minced celery
1/2 cup coarsely chopped ham
1 medium onion, finely chopped

1/4 teaspoon thyme leaves
Salt and pepper to taste
2 tablespoons butter

In a skillet, sauté onions, celery, ham, and thyme leaves in butter until limp. Add tomatoes and cook until limp. Add salt and pepper to taste. Pour mixture over poached eggs. Serve at once. Serves 6.

Vegetables

STUFFED CABBAGE

1 large head green cabbage   Salted water

Remove 12 large leaves of cabbage. Put leaves in large pot of salted boiling water and cook for 3 minutes or until slightly tender. Drain in colander.

STUFFING

1/2 pound uncooked hot Louisiana sausage, thinly sliced
2 cups corn bread, crumbled
1 medium onion, chopped

3 tablespoons margarine
5 ribs celery, chopped
1/4 teaspoon thyme leaves
2 tablespoons minced parsley
1 cup tomato sauce

Fry sausage in skillet until done. Drain on absorbent paper. In another skillet, melt margarine and sauté onions, celery, and parsley until limp. Add sausage and thyme leaves. Toss in corn bread, and coat well with vegetable mixture. Allow to cool. Flatten cabbage leaves. Put 2 tablespoons corn bread stuffing in each and fold up envelope style. Repeat until all leaves are stuffed. Grease 9 × 13-inch baking dish and put stuffed cabbage into it. Pour tomato sauce over top. Bake in 325°F oven for 30 minutes. Serves 6.

CANDIED CARROTS

8 large carrots, peeled and sliced in 1/2-inch rounds
6 tablespoons butter

1 cup sugar
2 lemons, thinly sliced
2 tablespoons lemon juice

In saucepan, put sliced carrots and cover with water. Bring to boil. Simmer about 15 minutes or until tender to fork. Drain carrots and put them in casserole dish. In skillet, heat butter, sugar, and lemon juice. Stir until thick and all sugar and butter is well blended. Continue to stir. Add lemon slices. If syrup becomes too thick, add a little water. Pour syrup over carrots. Bake in 350°F oven for 20 minutes. Serves 6.

• VEGETABLES •

ONION SOUFFLE

6 medium onions, peeled and cut in quarters
1/2 teaspoon salt
1/4 teaspoon white pepper
1/8 teaspoon Cayenne pepper
4 tablespoons butter

4 tablespoons flour
1/3 cup heavy cream
1/3 cup onion water
3 egg yolks, beaten slightly
3 egg whites, beaten very stiff
1-quart soufflé dish

Boil onions until very soft. Drain onions and reserve 1/3 cup water. Chop onions and drain again. Season with salt and peppers.

In top of double boiler over boiling water, mix butter, flour, cream, and 1/3 cup onion water. With wire whisk, blend thoroughly. Cook until sauce is thick. Add onion pulp and 3 egg yolks and blend well. Continue to cook until a very thick sauce. Remove from boiling water. Cool slightly. Carefully fold in stiffly beaten egg whites.

Turn mixture into soufflé dish. Bake in 375°F oven for 25 to 30 minutes. Serve at once. Serves 6.

ONION RINGS

3 large Bermuda onions
Chilled salted water
2/3 cup milk
1/2 cup flour

1 teaspoon cornstarch
Salt and pepper to taste
Oil for deep frying

Slice cleaned onions into 1/4-inch slices and separate into rings. Soak onion rings in chilled salted water for 30 minutes. Remove from water and dry. Combine flour and cornstarch with salt and pepper.

Dip onion rings in milk and then in seasoned flour until they are well coated.

In heavy skillet, place about 2 inches cooking oil. Heat oil to 375°F. Fry onion rings, a few at a time, until they are browned (about 3 minutes). Drain on absorbent paper. Serves 4.

• VEGETABLES •

BAKED ONIONS AND TOMATOES

3 large tomatoes, peeled
3 large white onions, peeled
1/2 cup seasoned bread crumbs
1 teaspoon seasoned salt and pepper
3 tablespoons grated Parmesan cheese
2 tablespoons melted butter

Slice onions very thin. Slice tomatoes very thin. In glass baking dish, about 9 × 13 inches and greased with butter, layer bottom with onion rings and cover with tomato slices. Sprinkle top with bread crumbs. Sprinkle bread crumbs with seasoned salt and pepper and cheese. Pour melted butter over crumbs. Bake in 375°F oven for 30 minutes or until crumbs bubble on top. Serves 6.

CREOLE TOMATOES PESTO

5 large tomatoes or Creole tomatoes
Butter
Bread crumbs
Pesto sauce

Peel and slice the tomatoes. Slices should be about 1/2 inch thick. Grease 8-inch square glass baking dish with butter. Place layer of sliced tomatoes on bottom, and dot each slice with 1/8 teaspoon pesto sauce. Cover layer with bread crumbs. Repeat until all slices are layered and dotted with pesto sauce and bread crumbs.

Place glass dish in center of microwave oven. On full power, cook for 3 minutes or until edges bubble, or broil in oven 3 inches from heat for about 5 minutes until done. Serve hot. Serves 6.

• 75 •
GRILLED TOMATOES

6 large Creole tomatoes
1 cup bread crumbs
1/2 cup grated cheddar cheese
1 tablespoon minced parsley

1/8 teaspoon sweet basil
Salt and pepper to taste
Butter

Slice a 1/4-inch slice off top of each tomato. Scrape inside pulp into bowl. Chop pulp. Mix pulp with all other ingredients except butter. Stuff tomato shells to top with mixture, and dot with butter. Place tomatoes in shallow baking dish and broil 4 inches from heat for about 5 to 7 minutes. Serves 6.

• 76 •
POTATO BALLS

1½ pounds peeled boiled potatoes
1/2 cup scalded milk
1/2 cup grated cheddar cheese
3 tablespoons melted butter
1/2 teaspoon salt

3 drops Tabasco
1 egg beaten with 1 teaspoon water
1 cup flavored bread crumbs
Cooking oil

In electric mixer, beat together potatoes, milk, butter, cheese, salt, and Tabasco. Beat until smooth and fluffy. Form into little balls (about 1½ inches in diameter). Dip balls in beaten egg and roll in bread crumbs. Coat well. In shallow baking dish, coat bottom with cooking oil. Preheat oven to 450°F. Bake balls for 5 minutes. Turn carefully with slotted spoon. Bake for additional 5 minutes or until browned. Serves 6.

CAULIFLOWER AU GRATIN

1 large head cauliflower

Boil cauliflower until just tender, or microwave on high power for 8 minutes. Break cauliflower into small florets. Put them in buttered casserole dish.

CHEESE SAUCE

2 tablespoons flour
2 tablespoons butter
1 cup milk

1 cup shredded cheddar cheese
Salt and pepper to taste
1/2 cup seasoned bread crumbs

In saucepan over medium heat, blend butter and flour. Add milk and wire-whisk it until smooth and a little thick. Add cheese, salt, and pepper, and continue to beat with wire whisk. Remove from heat.

TO ASSEMBLE: Pour cheese sauce over cauliflower. Sprinkle top with bread crumbs. Bake in 325°F oven for 20 minutes or until cheese sauce bubbles. Serves 6.

CREOLE STEWED CORN

2 cups fresh corn, cut from 6 to 8 cobs
3 large tomatoes, peeled and chopped
1 large onion, chopped
1/2 medium green pepper, chopped

4 tablespoons butter
1 teaspoon salt
1/2 teaspoon sugar
1/8 teaspoon black pepper

In skillet with cover, sauté onions in butter until limp. Add all other ingredients. Stir. Lower heat. Cover. Cook about 15 minutes, stirring every 5 minutes. Serves 6.

• VEGETABLES •

BROWN–WILD RICE CASSEROLE

2 cups wild rice, cooked
4 cups Louisiana brown rice, cooked
1 pound smoked sausage, thinly sliced
2 large chicken livers, coarsely chopped
1 medium onion, chopped
2 cups celery with tops, finely chopped
8 green onions with tops, finely chopped
1/2 cup minced parsley
1 stick butter
1/2 teaspoon thyme leaves
1/4 teaspoon poultry seasoning
1/4 teaspoon garlic powder
Salt and pepper to taste

In large skillet, sauté onions, celery, green onions, and parsley in 3/4 stick of butter until they are limp. Remove from heat.

In another large skillet, add remaining butter. Sauté livers until almost done. Add sausage. Continue to cook for 5 minutes.

Return vegetable skillet to heat and add thyme, poultry seasoning, garlic powder, and salt and pepper. Stir in sautéed liver and sausages. Blend well. Remove from heat.

Blend rices together with vegetable-sausage-liver mixture, coating well. Turn into buttered 2-quart casserole dish with cover. Bake covered for 25 minutes in 325°F oven. Serves 6 to 8.

• VEGETABLES •

STUFFED EGGPLANT

3 medium eggplants
1 pound shrimp, peeled, deveined, and chopped
1 large onion, chopped
3 ribs celery, chopped
3 tablespoons margarine

2 tablespoons chopped parsley
1 cup bread crumbs
1/4 cup grated Romano cheese
Salt and pepper to taste
1/8 teaspoon thyme leaves
Butter

In large pot, boil eggplant until tender to fork. Drain and set aside to cool. Split eggplants lengthwise and scrape out pulp, leaving 1/4 inch around sides. Chop pulp. Reserve shells for stuffing. In large skillet, melt margarine and sauté onions and celery for about 5 minutes. Add shrimp and continue to cook until shrimp turn pink. Add pulp, parsley, thyme leaves, salt, and pepper. Lower heat to lowest setting. Cook for 10 minutes. Cool. Stuff shells, heaping them full. Mix bread crumbs and Romano cheese. Sprinkle over tops of stuffed eggplant and dot with butter. Put stuffed eggplant in shallow baking dish. Bake in 300°F oven for 25 minutes. Serves 6.

Salads

MARDI GRAS SALAD

6 cups pasta twists, boiled and drained
2 cups shredded purple cabbage
1 large green pepper, seeded and chopped
1 cup canned yellow corn kernels, drained
1/4 cup chopped plain green olives
1 teaspoon yellow mustard
3/4 cup Creole mayonnaise
1/4 cup cider vinegar
Dash of dry sweet basil
Paprika
Lettuce

Combine vinegar, mayonnaise, and mustard in small bowl. Whisk together thoroughly. In another bowl, combine all other ingredients except lettuce and paprika. Toss well. Pour mayonnaise mixture over. Toss thoroughly. Cover bowl with plastic wrap and allow to ripen at room temperature for 1 hour. Uncover and toss again. Line salad bowl with lettuce leaves. Place pasta salad in bowl and sprinkle generously with paprika. Serves 6 to 8.

NEW POTATO SALAD

36 small new potatoes, boiled, peeled, and cooled
1 cup sour cream
1/2 cup thinly sliced celery
1/2 teaspoon horseradish
2 tablespoons lemon juice
1/8 teaspoon black pepper
1/4 cup fresh dill, chopped

In bowl, combine sour cream, celery, horseradish, lemon juice, pepper, and dill. Blend well. Add potatoes and toss, coating thoroughly. Refrigerate for 2 hours. Serves 6.

• SALADS •

COLESLAW

1 2-pound head of cabbage
4 large carrots, peeled

1/2 cup cubed pineapple

In food processor, with shredder plate, shred cabbage and carrots. In large bowl, blend cabbage, carrots, and pineapple and set aside.

BOILED DRESSING

3 eggs, beaten lightly
1/2 cup cider vinegar
1/3 cup water
3 tablespoons sugar
1 tablespoon flour

1 tablespoon cornstarch
2 teaspoons dry mustard
1 teaspoon salt
1 tablespoon margarine
1/2 cup milk

In 3-cup saucepan, combine vinegar, water, cornstarch, salt, flour, sugar, and mustard. Beat with wire whisk until smooth. Place sauce over medium heat. Add milk and margarine, whisking until mixture comes to boil. Remove from heat. Into beaten eggs, add about 4 tablespoons of boiled mixture and blend well. Add egg mixture to saucepan and return to heat. Continue to whisk until mixture is thick and smooth. Remove from heat and cool to room temperature.

Pour boiled dressing over cabbage-carrot-pineapple mixture. Toss thoroughly until well coated. Cover with plastic wrap and refrigerate 3 hours. Toss again before serving. Serves 6.

· 84 ·
CORN-TOMATO SALAD

3 cups whole kernel corn, cooked and drained
2 large tomatoes, peeled, seeded, and diced
1 medium onion, finely chopped
3 green onions, thinly sliced
2 tablespoons minced parsley
2 tablespoons lemon juice
1/4 teaspoon black pepper
1/4 teaspoon seasoned salt
1/4 teaspoon garlic salt
1/2 cup homemade Creole mayonnaise
Lettuce

In small bowl, blend together lemon juice, salts, pepper, and mayonnaise. In another bowl, mix corn, tomatoes, onions, and parsley. Toss. Pour dressing over corn mixture and toss again thoroughly. Serve on lettuce leaf. Serves 6.

· 85 ·
AVOCADO WITH CRABMEAT

3 large ripe avocados
1 pound white lump crabmeat
1/4 cup chopped onion
1/2 cup minced celery
1/2 cup mayonnaise
1 tablespoon minced parsley
3 tablespoons lemon juice
2 tablespoons capers
Salt and pepper to taste
Paprika
Lettuce

Split avocados in half lengthwise. Remove pits and discard. Peel avocados. Put crabmeat in mixing bowl. Pick through for shells, and discard them. Blend in mayonnaise, lemon juice, onion, celery, parsley, and capers. Toss to coat. Add salt and pepper. Toss again. Fill avocado shells with crabmeat mixture, mounding up. Sprinkle paprika on top. Serve each half on lettuce leaf. Serves 6.

NECTARINE-RICE SALAD

3 medium ripe nectarines, peeled and sliced
2 cups brown rice, cooked and cooled
2 tablespoons lemon juice
2 tablespoons honey
1/2 cup sour cream
2 ribs celery, thinly sliced
1/2 cup chopped pecans
Lettuce

In bowl, blend together sour cream, lemon juice, honey, and celery. Add rice, nectarines, and pecans. Mix well to coat. Serve on lettuce leaf. Serves 6.

SEAFOOD SALAD

24 boiled shrimp, peeled and deveined
1 hard-boiled egg, peeled and chopped
1/2 cup crabmeat
4 green onions with tops, chopped
3 cups shredded green cabbage
2 cups shredded lettuce
1 cup shredded spinach
1 cup croutons
3 tablespoons bacon bits

DRESSING

1 large egg
3 tablespoons lemon juice
1 cup salad oil
1/2 tablespoon Creole mustard
1/2 teaspoon salt
4 tablespoons half-and-half cream
1 tablespoon minced parsley

For dressing put egg, lemon juice, and 1/4 cup salad oil in blender. Blend at high speed for 10 seconds. Add mustard, salt, parsley, and cream. Blend at high speed for 5 seconds. With motor running, add remainder of oil in steady stream.

TO ASSEMBLE: Toss all salad ingredients in large salad bowl. Pour dressing over, tossing and coating well. Cover bowl with plastic wrap. Allow to stand at room temperature for 30 minutes before serving. Serves 6 to 8.

SHRIMP SALAD

2 pounds fresh or frozen shrimp
1 teaspoon liquid crab-shrimp boil

1 lemon, sliced
Lettuce

Boil shrimp in crab-shrimp boil, with lemon slices, about 10 minutes or until done. Turn off heat and allow shrimp to steep in water about 10 minutes. Drain. Cool. Peel and devein.

DRESSING

1 hard-boiled egg, peeled and cut in quarters
1 small onion, peeled and cut in quarters
1 rib celery, coarsely chopped
1 clove garlic, mashed
1/3 cup red wine vinegar
1/3 cup olive oil

1/3 cup dry white wine
1 large tomato, peeled and cut in quarters
1 teaspoon Creole mustard
1/2 teaspoon salt
1 drop bitters
2 drops Tabasco

Put all dressing ingredients into food processor with steel blades. Process until smooth and thick.

TO ASSEMBLE: In large bowl, toss shrimp with dressing until well coated. Cover bowl. Refrigerate for 2 hours. Serve in salad bowl lined with lettuce or on individual salad plates on lettuce leaf. Serves 6.

EGGPLANT-SHRIMP SALAD

2 medium eggplants
12 boiled shrimp, peeled, deveined, and chopped
2 large tomatoes, cut in small pieces

In preheated 400°F oven, cover eggplants in foil and bake for 40 minutes. Allow to cool to room temperature. Peel eggplants and cut flesh into 1/2-inch cubes. Toss eggplant, shrimp, and tomatoes in salad bowl.

DRESSING

1/3 cup olive oil
1/3 cup salad oil
1/3 cup red wine vinegar
1/2 teaspoon salt
1 clove garlic, mashed
1/8 teaspoon black pepper
1 teaspoon minced parsley

Combine all dressing ingredients in electric blender. Blend 45 seconds at high speed until creamy.

Pour dressing over salad and toss to coat well. Cover bowl with plastic wrap. Allow to stand at room temperature for 30 minutes. Toss again before serving. Serves 6 to 8.

HOT CHICKEN SALAD

3 boneless, skinless breasts of chicken, sliced in 1/2-inch strips
Salt and pepper
Flour
Cooking oil
2 large Granny Smith apples, peeled and diced
1/2 cup minced celery
1/2 cup coarsely chopped walnuts
1/4 cup lemon juice
1/2 cup honey
1/8 teaspoon salt
1/4 cup salad oil
1 teaspoon poppy seed

Salt and pepper chicken and dredge in flour. In skillet, heat 1/4 inch cooking oil. Brown chicken. Lower heat and continue to cook about 10 minutes or until done. Remove and drain on absorbent paper.

In small mixing bowl, whisk together honey, lemon juice, salt, salad oil, and poppy seed, blending thoroughly.

In another mixing bowl, put apples, celery, chicken, and walnuts. Pour dressing over them and toss to coat well. Serve warm on lettuce leaf. Serves 6.

Desserts

PINEAPPLE UPSIDE-DOWN SPONGE CAKE

7 slices canned pineapple
1/2 cup Maraschino cherries (about 14)
2 tablespoons melted butter
1/2 cup brown sugar, firmly packed
3/4 cup cake flour
1½ teaspoons baking powder
1/8 teaspoon salt
2 large eggs
1/2 cup white sugar
1½ tablespoons pineapple juice
1 9-inch cake pan

Spread bottom of 9-inch cake pan with melted butter and sprinkle with brown sugar. Arrange pineapple in a nice design, placing cherries in empty spaces. Sift flour, baking powder, and salt. Beat eggs with rotary beater until thick, yellow, and fluffy. Add white sugar to eggs and continue to beat. Add sifted dry ingredients and pineapple juice to egg mixture, beating until well blended. Pour over pineapple slices and cherries. Cover evenly, using rubber spatula. Bake in 350°F oven for 30 minutes or until cake tests done. Remove from oven and allow to cool in pan on a rack for 10 minutes. Loosen edges and turn out on serving plate. Serve warm. Serves 6.

STRAWBERRY SHORTCAKE

4 cups fresh whole strawberries
Sugar to sweeten

1 cup heavy cream, beaten very stiff
1 teaspoon Kirsch (optional)

Wash strawberries in colander and drain thoroughly. Remove green stems. Reserve 8 large strawberries. Cut remaining strawberries into thin slices. Put sliced strawberries in a bowl and sprinkle sugar over them until they are lightly coated. Let stand for 45 minutes.

SHORTCAKE

2 cups sifted enriched flour
3 teaspoons baking powder
1/2 cup shortening

3 tablespoons sugar
1/2 teaspoon salt
3/4 cup milk

Sift flour, sugar, salt, and baking powder 3 times in bowl. Cut in shortening with a pastry blender until mixture is grainy. Add milk all at once and mix lightly with a fork. Do not overmix. In a greased and floured 8-inch cake pan, spread dough uniformly with a rubber spatula. Bake in a 450°F oven for 20 to 25 minutes until golden brown. Remove at once from pan, and cool on a wire cake rack. Allow to cool for 10 minutes. Split cake crosswise with knife or sewing thread.

TO ASSEMBLE: Place bottom half of cake on serving tray. Spread generously with sliced strawberries and juice. Allow to stand 5 minutes. Place remaining layer on top, pressing it down gently to make a good fit. Fold Kirsch into whipped cream until well mixed. Top shortcake with whipped cream and garnish with whole strawberries evenly spaced on the outer side. Serves 8.

CASSATA ORLEANS

1 fresh pound cake (about 9 inches long and 4 inches wide)
1/2 pound fresh ricotta cheese
1/2 cup sugar
2 tablespoons heavy cream
3 tablespoons Grand Marnier
4 tablespoons coarsely chopped crystallized pineapple
1 oz. grated semisweet chocolate

With sharp knife or thread, cut pound cake horizontally, making 5 slices about 1/2 inch thick. Rub ricotta cheese into a bowl through a coarse sieve, with a wooden spoon. Combine cream, sugar, and Grand Marnier with ricotta cheese and beat until smooth. Fold in chocolate and pineapple. Place bottom slice on cake plate and spread ricotta mixture over the surface. Carefully add another slice, and repeat until all slices are coated, ending with plain slice on top. Chill cake in refrigerator for 2 hours until cake and filling remain firm.

FROSTING

1/4 cup butter or margarine, melted
1/3 cup cocoa
1/4 teaspoon salt
1/3 cup strong black coffee
1½ teaspoons vanilla extract
3½ cups sifted powdered sugar

Combine melted butter or margarine with salt, coffee, cocoa, and vanilla extract in a bowl. With electric beater, mix in sugar in 3 parts, beating until smooth and creamy. Frosting should be of spreading consistency. Do not overbeat.

Frost cake on all sides with small metal spatula, reserving about 1/3 of frosting for decorations of rosebuds. Make rosebuds on cake with decorator's pastry tube. Cover frosted cake loosely with aluminum foil. Refrigerate for 24 hours to allow cassata to ripen. Makes about 10 slices.

ZABAGLIONE A LA CREOLE

6 egg yolks
1 cup sugar
1 teaspoon grated orange rind
1¼ cups sweet white wine
1/2 teaspoon vanilla extract
4 tablespoons white rum
1 cup stiffly beaten whipped cream
12 ladyfingers
6 sherbert glasses

In the top of a double boiler, whisk together sugar, eggs, and vanilla until the mixture forms ribbons. Put top of boiler over boiling water and whisk in the rum, white wine, and grated orange rind, whisking vigorously until mixture becomes frothy and stiff. Remove from boiling water and cool slightly. Fold in whipped cream.

TO ASSEMBLE: Crumble ladyfingers, and place about 1/2 inch in the bottom of each glass. Pour zabaglione over. Garnish tops with remaining ladyfinger crumbs. Serve warm. Serves 6.

BROWNIE WAFFLES A LA MODE

1½ cups sifted enriched flour
1/2 teaspoon salt
2/3 cup sugar
1 teaspoon baking powder
2 egg yolks
3/4 cup milk
2 egg whites, beaten very stiff
3/4 cup cooking oil
2 squares unsweetened chocolate, melted
1/2 cup chopped pecans
Vanilla ice cream
Chocolate syrup

Sift flour, salt, sugar, and baking powder in a bowl. Beat egg yolks and milk together. Add egg-milk mixture to sifted ingredients and beat thoroughly. Add cooking oil and melted chocolate and beat in completely. Fold in chopped pecans and egg whites. Bake at medium heat in a waffle iron for about 5 minutes or until steam no longer appears. Remove and cool on wire rack.

Divide waffle into 6 pieces. Serve each with a generous scoop of vanilla ice cream topped with chocolate syrup. Serves 6.

• DESSERTS •

PRALINE PARFAIT

2 pints French vanilla ice cream
1 cup whipping cream
1 teaspoon sugar

6 parfait glasses, or 6 large bowl-shaped wine glasses

Whip cream until very stiff, and fold in sugar. Cover and refrigerate.

PRALINE SAUCE

1 cup dark brown sugar
1/2 cup white sugar
1/2 cup water
1/2 cup whipping cream

1½ cups pecan halves
2 teaspoons vanilla extract
1/4 teaspoon salt

In heavy skillet over medium heat, combine both sugars, water, and salt. Dissolve sugar well. Add cream. Continue to cook to just under boiling point, about 200°F on a candy thermometer. Remove from heat and beat in vanilla extract and pecan halves. Cool but do not refrigerate.

TO ASSEMBLE: Pour small amount of praline sauce in bottom of each glass. Put small scoop of ice cream in each glass. Pour more sauce over ice cream. Add another scoop and more praline sauce. Top with the chilled whipped cream. Serves 6.

CANTALOUPE A LA MODE

3 large ripe cantaloupes
2 pints French vanilla ice cream
1/2 cup sugar

1/4 cup water
1/4 cup Kirsch
6 sprigs fresh mint

Cut cantaloupes in half. Remove all seeds. Reserve shells. Make melon balls with melon-ball scoop. Place balls in glass or plastic bowl. In saucepan, dissolve sugar and water. Remove from heat. Add Kirsch. Stir. Cool. Pour Kirsch mixture over melon balls. Toss. Cover with plastic wrap and refrigerate for 2 hours.

TO ASSEMBLE: Fill each shell with melon balls. Top with generous scoop of ice cream. Garnish each shell with mint sprig. Serves 6.

• DESSERTS •

MILE HIGH PIE

1 9-inch pie shell, baked and cooled
1 pint French vanilla ice cream
1 pint chocolate ice cream
8 egg whites
1/4 teaspoon vanilla extract
1/4 teaspoon almond extract
1/2 teaspoon cream of tartar
Pinch of salt
1/2 cup powdered sugar

Layer vanilla ice cream in shell. Layer chocolate ice cream over. Put in freezer. Beat egg whites with cream of tartar and salt until stiff. Gradually add sugar and extracts, and continue to beat until meringue is glossy. Heat broiler of oven. Cover ice cream completely with meringue to edges of pie shell. Broil for 30 to 45 seconds under broiler or until meringue sets and is golden. Put in freezer for 2 to 3 hours.

CHOCOLATE SAUCE

2 oz. German sweet chocolate
2 oz. unsweetened chocolate
4 oz. heavy whipping cream
1/2 cup sugar
1 tablespoon brandy

In double boiler over boiling water, add both chocolates, sugar, brandy, and 2 oz. cream. Melt mixture and allow to thicken. Wire-whisk in remaining cream. Remove from heat. Slice pie into 8 equal portions. Serve with chocolate sauce drizzled over meringue. Serves 8.

PINEAPPLE-BANANA CANAPE

6 slices (1/2 inch thick) white bread
1 cup fresh or canned pineapple cubes, drained
1 large underripe banana, sliced
1/2 cup Maraschino cherries, drained
1/2 cup light brown sugar mixed with 1 teaspoon ground cinnamon
Softened butter

Coat each slice of bread with softened butter. Sprinkle with some sugar mixture. Arrange slices on cookie sheet. Arrange pineapple, banana slices, and cherries on each slice. Sprinkle with more sugar mixture. Dot with butter. In preheated broiler, broil about 6 inches from heat for 5 to 7 minutes or until well grilled and bread is toasted. Serve as dessert or side dish with fowl or pork. Serves 6.

PEACHES IN CHAMPAGNE

6 large fresh peaches
1 cup sugar
Water
1/2 cup Napoleon brandy
24 whole cloves
1 bottle chilled champagne
6 sherbert glasses

Peel peaches and leave them whole. Press 4 cloves into each peach. Place peaches in large saucepan. Pour sugar over them and cover with water. Bring peaches to a boil. Add brandy. Lower heat and simmer until peaches are tender to a fork. Drain peaches and remove cloves. Put peaches in covered bowl and refrigerate for 4 to 6 hours. Place a peach in a sherbert glass and fill glass with chilled champagne. Serve with cookies. Serves 6.

• DESSERTS •

FRESH PEACH COBBLER

2 cups all-purpose flour
1 teaspoon salt
2/3 cup shortening
6 tablespoons ice water

In mixing bowl, sift flour and salt together. Cut in shortening with pastry blender. Sprinkle with water. Mix well. Divide pastry into 2/3 and 1/3. Roll both portions out on floured board. In a round 10 × 2-inch deep glass baking dish, fit bottom with the larger portion of rolled out pastry.

FILLING

4 cups fresh ripe peaches, peeled and sliced
3/4 cup sugar
1/8 teaspoon salt
2½ tablespoons cornstarch
1/8 teaspoon almond extract
1/2 cup slivered almonds
Whipped cream for topping

In mixing bowl, mix sugar, salt, and cornstarch. Sprinkle peaches with almond extract. Add slivered almonds. Gently toss together peaches and cornstarch-sugar mixture. Fill pastry shell.

With remaining dough, cut 5/8-inch strips and form a lattice on top of peaches. Secure ends of dough, and flute. Bake in 425°F oven for 15 to 20 minutes. Reduce heat to 325°F and continue to bake for 25 to 30 minutes or until crust is golden brown. Allow to cool until just warm. Serve warm with whipped cream topping. Serves 6 to 8.

• 102 •
GRANDMOTHER'S OMELETTE SOUFFLE

2 egg yolks
2 egg whites
2 teaspoons cracker meal
2 teaspoons sugar

Few grains salt
Pinch of cream of tartar
1 teaspoon butter

In a small bowl, cream together egg yolks, sugar, and cracker meal. In another bowl, beat egg whites with salt and cream of tartar with rotary beater until stiff and fluffy. Fold egg yolk mixture gently into stiff egg whites. Heat butter to bubbling point in omelette pan or 8-inch skillet. Heap mixture in center of pan and gently smooth it out. Lower heat to medium, and cook until a golden crust appears. Turn with care. Cook until crust forms again. Center should be slightly firm. Serve at once. Serves 1.

• 103 •
YAM PUDDING

3 very large Louisiana yams, peeled
Salted water
1/2 cup sugar
1 stick butter

3 large eggs
10 oz. evaporated milk
1/8 teaspoon cinnamon
Whipped cream for topping

Place yams in saucepan and cover with salted water. Boil until very tender, about 30 minutes. Drain. In food processor, place yams, sugar, and butter. Process until smooth. Add eggs one at a time through funnel while processor is on. Add cinnamon to milk. In a steady stream, process in milk. The mixture should have a runny consistency. Pour mixture into 4-cup baking or soufflé dish. Bake in 325°F oven for 50 to 60 minutes or until a knife blade inserted comes out clean. Cool to warm temperature. Serve with whipped cream topping. Serves 6.

• DESSERTS •

GINGERBREAD

1/2 cup freshly brewed coffee with chicory
1/2 cup boiling water
2 sticks butter, softened
1 cup light brown sugar, firmly packed
1 cup dark molasses
3 eggs

2½ cups sifted flour
1½ teaspoons baking soda
1/2 teaspoon salt
1 teaspoon ground cinnamon
1/8 teaspoon nutmeg
1/8 teaspoon ground cloves
1 teaspoon ground ginger

In large electric mixer bowl, cream together sugar and butter. Add boiling water and coffee, alternating with flour and baking soda. Add salt. Add molasses and spices. Add eggs one at a time. Mix for 2 minutes until smooth.

Pour batter into 9 × 13-inch greased and floured baking dish. Bake for 1 hour at 325°F. Cool in pan for 15 minutes. Remove and cut into squares. Serve with sweetened whipped cream or vanilla ice cream. Serves 10.

BANANA-PECAN BREAD

1 stick softened butter
1/2 cup white sugar
1/4 cup light brown sugar
3 large ripe bananas, mashed
2 large beaten eggs

2 cups flour
2 teaspoons baking powder
1/2 teaspoon salt
1/2 cup chopped pecans
1/2 teaspoon vanilla extract

Cream butter and sugars in electric mixer. Add bananas, eggs, and vanilla extract. Add flour, salt, and baking powder. Fold in chopped pecans.

Pour batter into well-greased and floured loaf pan. Preheat oven to 325°F. Bake bread for 60 to 70 minutes, or until tester comes out clean. Remove bread from pan after 10 minutes' cooling time. When completely cooled, wrap in waxed paper and allow to ripen for 24 hours before slicing and serving. This bread is excellent toasted and served with breakfast foods. Makes 1 loaf.

HONEY-PECAN BREAD

1 cup honey
1 cup milk
1/2 cup sugar
2 egg yolks
4 tablespoons softened butter
2½ cups sifted flour
1 teaspoon baking soda
1/4 teaspoon salt
1/2 teaspoon vanilla extract
3/4 cup coarsely chopped pecans

In saucepan, scald milk. Add honey and sugar and stir until dissolved. Cool mixture.

In mixing bowl, cream eggs and butter until smooth; add flour, baking soda, and salt, and blend well. Beat in honey mixture and vanilla extract. Fold in pecans. Pour batter into greased and floured bread loaf pan.

Bake in slow oven 325°F for 55 to 60 minutes or until it tests done. Cool in bread pan for 15 minutes and turn out on a wire rack. Serve thinly sliced with cream cheese and strawberry preserves. Makes 1 loaf.

LEMON LADYFINGERS

24 single ladyfingers

Powdered sugar

LEMON CURD

8 tablespoons butter
1/2 cup sugar
1/4 cup fresh lemon juice
2 teaspoons grated lemon rind
3 well-beaten eggs

Heat heavy saucepan. Melt butter and sugar with lemon juice. Add small amount of butter mixture to eggs. Blend well. Transfer back to saucepan. Whisk well. Whisking constantly, allow sauce to thicken. Beat in lemon rind. Remove from heat as soon as curd comes to bubble. Pour lemon curd in small glass bowl. Cover with plastic wrap. Refrigerate for 1 hour.

TO ASSEMBLE: Coat bottom side of ladyfinger with lemon curd. Press another ladyfinger on top. Repeat until all ladyfingers are used. Sprinkle generously with powdered sugar. Serve with ice cream or as a tea cookie. Makes 12.

• DESSERTS •

Lagniappe

BREAKFAST CORN BREAD MUFFINS

1 cup yellow corn meal
1 cup flour
1 large egg
1 cup milk
1/3 cup sugar

4 teaspoons baking powder
1/4 cup corn oil
Strawberry jam
Powdered sugar

Combine flour, corn meal, sugar, and baking powder in mixing bowl. Beat egg into milk. Add corn oil to milk mixture. Add mixture to dry ingredients. Beat until fairly smooth. Fill well-greased muffin tin compartments about 2/3 full. Preheat oven to 450°F. Bake 15 to 20 minutes.

Remove muffins to cooling rack. Split muffins crosswise. Remove small amount of crumbs from center. Fill depression with 1/2 teaspoon strawberry jam. Press muffin tops and bottoms together. Dust tops with powdered sugar. Serve warm. Makes 1 dozen.

GINGERBREAD WAFFLES

1/3 cup liquid margarine
1 cup dark molasses
2 egg yolks
2 egg whites, beaten very stiff
2 cups sifted flour
1/2 teaspoon baking soda

2 teaspoons baking powder
1/2 cup milk
1 teaspoon ground cinnamon
1 teaspoon ground ginger
1/2 teaspoon salt
1/2 cup chopped pecans

In mixing bowl, whisk together molasses, milk, yolks, and liquid margarine. Sift together flour, salt, cinnamon, ginger, baking soda, and baking powder. Beat into molasses mixture. Fold in egg whites and pecans.

Heat waffle iron. Pour enough batter to bake proper-sized waffle. Bake until iron stops steaming. Do not overbake. Serve with powdered sugar as breakfast fare, or with whipped cream or ice cream as dessert. Makes 12 small or 6 large waffles.

• LAGNIAPPE •

· 110 ·
GARLIC POPOVERS

1 cup sifted flour
1/2 teaspoon salt
2 large eggs
1 cup milk

1 tablespoon salad oil
1 tablespoon garlic purée
1/2 tablespoon minced parsley

In a bowl, whisk together milk and eggs. Add flour, salt, garlic purée, and parsley. Blend well. Beat in salad oil.

Generously grease large custard cups or muffin tin. Fill 1/2 full with batter. Bake in 400°F oven for 35 to 40 minutes. Caution: Do not open door during cooking. Remove at once. Serve hot with butter. Makes 6 to 8 popovers.

· 111 ·
HUSH PUPPIES

2 cups yellow corn meal
1 cup all-purpose flour
2 tablespoons baking powder
1 large beaten egg
2 teaspoons sugar

1 teaspoon seasoned salt
1 tablespoon onion purée
1 tablespoon minced parsley
Milk
Cooking oil

Mix all ingredients except milk and oil in bowl. Add just enough milk to make a thick dough. Coat fingers with oil, and roll dough into balls the size of a golf ball. Fry in oil about 375°F, turning until brown on all sides. Remove and drain on absorbent paper. Serves 6.

MUFFULETTA SANDWICH

7-inch round loaf of Italian Cap bread with sesame seeds
1/4 pound sliced smoked ham
1/4 pound sliced salami

1/4 pound sliced provolone cheese
1/2 cup Italian olive salad, chopped

TO ASSEMBLE: Slice round loaf in half crosswise. Remove some soft crumbs to form thick shells (this will help contain the olive salad). Discard crumbs. Place bottom part of bread on plate. Spread with 1/2 the olive salad. Place ham over salad. Put cheese over ham. Put salami over cheese. Top with remainder of olive salad. Put top bread lid on. Slice like a pie, into 6 equal slices. Serves 6.

NOTE: The spelling of "muffuletta" varies in New Orleans. At the time of this writing, this spelling appears on the sign of the Central Grocery, 923 Decatur Street, across from the French Market. Central Grocery claims the origination of this sandwich.

ALL-PURPOSE SEASONING

1 26-oz. box plain salt
4 tablespoons Cayenne pepper
3 tablespoons black pepper
3 tablespoons chili powder
3 tablespoons garlic powder

2 tablespoons onion powder
1 teaspoon nutmeg
3/4 teaspoon ground thyme
1 tablespoon monosodium glutamate (optional)

Mix all ingredients in large bowl. Blend well. Store in airtight glass container. Use in amounts according to taste. Makes 1 quart.

• 114 •
HOMEMADE CREOLE MAYONNAISE

1 cup salad oil
1/2 teaspoon dry mustard
1 large egg
1/2 teaspoon seasoned salt

2 tablespoons cider vinegar
1/2 teaspoon Creole mustard
1/4 teaspoon garlic powder

Break egg into blender. Add dry mustard, salt, vinegar, and garlic powder. Add 1/2 cup oil. On low speed, blend well for 5 seconds. Remove top; add remainder of oil in a steady stream. When all oil is consumed, turn blender to highest speed for 5 seconds. Fold in Creole mustard. Makes about 1½ cups.

• 115 •
CREOLE FRENCH DRESSING

1½ cups salad oil
3/4 cup cider vinegar
1 teaspoon seasoned salt
1/8 teaspoon black pepper

1/4 cup ketchup
1 teaspoon Worcestershire sauce
3 cloves garlic, mashed

Place all ingredients in blender. Blend at low speed for 10 seconds. Makes 2 cups.

• LAGNIAPPE •

ALL-PURPOSE CAJUN BARBECUE SAUCE

2 large onions, peeled and cut in quarters
2 large cloves garlic
1 teaspoon chili powder
2 cups fresh or canned tomatoes, peeled and chopped
1 teaspoon dry mustard
1/4 cup dark brown sugar
1/2 teaspoon salt
1/2 cup dry red wine
1 cup cooking oil
1/2 cup fresh lemon juice
1/2 teaspoon black pepper
1/2 teaspoon Tabasco
1/2 teaspoon each, celery seed and thyme leaves
1/2 cup water

Put all ingredients in food processor with steel blade. Process until completely puréed. Pour mixture in saucepan and bring to boil. Lower heat to simmer. Cook for 10 minutes. Remove from heat and cool. Store in glass jar in refrigerator.

Excellent with spare ribs, chicken, sausage, beef, or lamb. Makes 3 cups.

PESTO SAUCE LOUISIANE

1 cup fresh parsley with stems removed
1 cup fresh spinach with stems removed
1/4 cup fresh sweet basil with stems removed
2 large cloves garlic, peeled
1/2 cup olive oil
1/4 teaspoon salt
1/4 teaspoon black pepper
1/3 cup grated Parmesan cheese
1/4 cup chopped pecans

Wash parsley, spinach, and basil and drain well. Put in food processor with steel blade. Process until smooth and well minced. Add garlic, salt, pepper, and cheese. With processor running, pour olive oil into food chute in steady stream until well mixed. Fold in pecans until well blended.

Sauce can be used immediately, or refrigerated in airtight container for up to 1 month. Can be frozen and stored for 6 months. Makes 1¾ cups.

· 118 ·
REMOULADE SAUCE CREOLE

1 cup olive oil
1 teaspoon dry mustard
1/2 cup ketchup
1 teaspoon sugar
1 tablespoon paprika
2 teaspoons salt
1/4 cup wine vinegar

1/8 cup horseradish
1 tablespoon minced parsley
3 green onions with tops, finely chopped
1 rip celery, minced
6 drops Tabasco

Put all ingredients in blender; blend well. Allow to ripen for 4 hours in refrigerator. Sauce can be stored in refrigerator for 2 weeks. Makes 2 cups.

· 119 ·
ALL-PURPOSE CREOLE TOMATO SAUCE

1 pound fresh or canned tomatoes, peeled, seeded, and chopped
1/3 cup cooking oil
1 large onion, minced
4 ribs celery, finely chopped
4 cloves garlic, mashed
3 tablespoons minced parsley
6 oz. tomato paste

1 cup beef stock
1 teaspoon sugar
1½ teaspoons salt
1/8 teaspoon black pepper
1/8 teaspoon crushed red pepper
3 large bay leaves
1/8 teaspoon thyme leaves
4 cups boiling water

In large skillet that has a cover, sauté onions and celery in cooking oil until limp. Add tomatoes and continue to cook over medium heat for about 5 minutes. Add beef stock, garlic, parsley, salt, peppers, thyme, and bay leaves. Continue to cook for 5 minutes. Lower heat to lowest setting. Stir mixture to keep from sticking. Add tomato paste and sugar with boiling water. Blend well. Cover skillet and cook for 2 hours. This sauce should be stirred every 15 minutes for best results. Cool and store in glass container in refrigerator for future use. Use within 7 days of preparation. Remove bay leaves before serving. Makes about 4½ cups.

· LAGNIAPPE ·

ALL-PURPOSE SAUCE PIQUANTE

6 cups canned stewed tomatoes, chopped (reserve juice)
1 cup finely chopped celery
8 green onions with tops, finely chopped
1 cup minced parsley
10 cloves minced garlic
1 cup onion purée
2 tablespoons flour
2 tablespoons cooking oil
1 teaspoon Cayenne pepper
1 teaspoon salt
Juice of 1 lemon
Grated rind of 1 lemon
1 cup water

In saucepan, make a roux with flour and oil. Develop roux to medium brown color. Add all other ingredients to saucepan. Bring to boil. Lower heat to just under boiling point. Cover and cook for 30 minutes. The sauce is very hot and spicy. Can be used on fish, shellfish, fowl, or beef. Store in glass container in refrigerator. Will last about 4 weeks. Makes 4 to 6 cups.

CHOCOLATE SAUCE

3 oz. unsweetened chocolate
3 oz. German sweet chocolate
3/4 cup heavy whipping cream
3/4 cup sugar
1 teaspoon vanilla extract

In double boiler over boiling water, melt chocolates, sugar, and 1/2 of whipping cream. Remove from heat. With wire whisk, beat in remainder of cream and vanilla extract. Cool to room temperature. Makes about 1½ cups.

• LAGNIAPPE •